"I loved reading this book! *The Little Book of Big Change* will help the field of addictions and anyone suffering from a debilitating habit to find an easier, more enlightened path to full recovery, not only from habits and addictions, but a recovery of the innate health that is all of our birthright. I will encourage all the treatment centers I work with to use this as a course book for treatment. Johnson has moved the field forward to a new paradigm of treatment and recovery from addictions."

—**Joseph Bailey, MA, LP**, licensed psychologist,
   author of *The Serenity Principle*, and coauthor
   of *Slowing Down to the Speed of Life*

"The clarity, wisdom, and practicality of this book are simply extraordinary and unmatched in the field of addiction, making it the absolute number one read for anyone struggling with or treating destructive habits. A powerful and radiant light that brings instant relief, hope, and peace of mind."

—**Erika Bugbee, MA**, partner and cofounder
   of the Online Learning Division at Pransky
   & Associates

"*The Little Book of Big Change* is going to be a game changer for my counseling practice. I can't wait to share this book with my clients. Amy writes in such a simple, commonsense way about what's behind all habits…whether behaviors or thoughts that we would like to see change. It is a 'one-size-fits-all' kind of book. I see big changes ahead for all who read this book (including myself)!"

—**Karen Miller Williams**, Three Principles
practitioner and mental well-being expert for over
thirty-five years, emotional well-being educator,
counselor, coach, and consultant

"This book completely overturns current ideas about addiction, the people who suffer with them, and the human ability for change. Amy not only provides hope and a simple solution for eliminating addictive behaviors, she offers a profoundly hopeful look at the ability we *all* have to feel more at peace in life."

—**Mara Gleason, MSW**, cofounder of One Thought,
a leading global company that helps individuals and
businesses unleash their greatest potential through
clear thinking

"I love this groundbreaking book! It frees people from the misguided idea that breaking self-destructive habits takes willpower, 'bootstrap pulling,' tools, techniques, or thought reconditioning! It helps people see the innocence of their self-defeating habits so they can let go of guilt and blame. It helps people realize that they have all the mental health they need already inside of them. It shows people how to use the power of thought in their best interest. When people grasp these new insights, their habits naturally melt away."

—**Thomas M. Kelley, PhD**, associate professor at Wayne State University, and licensed psychologist

"When Amy Johnson speaks of spirituality in this book, she is not playing lightly. Johnson speaks of a spirituality that both moves the universe and is also at the heart of ending addiction. This book reveals psychospiritual principles that are the essence of all spiritual teachings, and finally, tie spirit and science together. The information in this book can free you not just from addiction to behaviors, but from addiction to thoughts, the real culprit! A clear, profound, well-written, and revolutionary book."

—**Ami Chen Mills-Naim**, author of *The Spark Inside* and *State of Mind in the Classroom*, and founder of Ami Chen Coaching and Education

"Thanks to this powerful book, I've been Googling 'How to Build a Time Machine,' because, my gosh, I would have *loved* this book back when my worst addiction (habit) was ruining me, but I find now it also works, as a system, to delete even the smallest of current annoying habits! Very highly recommended!"

—**Steve Chandler**, author of *Time Warrior*

"Amy's potentially life-changing book gets right to the heart of who we really are: spiritual beings already and always healthy at our core. Amy's presentation of the spiritual understanding of the Three Principles provides genuine hope that everyone already has what it takes to be free of their addictions and habits!"

—**Dicken Bettinger, EdD**, retired licensed psychologist, and founder of Three Principles Mentoring

"Combining modern neuroscience with timeless spiritual principles, Amy Johnson delivers a new understanding of habits that is both fascinating and practical, liberating and simple. She explains why harmful habits aren't powerful, stable parts of who we are, but temporary logjams that cloud our natural state of well-being. Johnson helps her readers put aside faulty thoughts and urges, and points them toward the guidance of their innate wisdom. Anyone with a harmful behavioral or mental habit needs to read this book!"

—**Kathryn Hansen**, author of *Brain over Binge*

"Absolutely brilliant! *The Little Book of Big Change* is a game changer and is now officially one of my favorite self-help books. Authentic, gentle, and wise, Johnson masterfully leads us to life-changing insights—it's impossible to read this book and not immediately feel better in a long-lasting, 'I see,' way. If you're stuck on some habit, read this book! You will likely get more than you can imagine."

—**Lisa Esile**, coauthor of *Whose Mind Is It Anyway?*

"This book is the antidote to self-help; a powerful and insightfully written explanation of how we as human beings create our perceptions of the world we live in and how we live out those experiences and habits. Amy Johnson describes a new understanding of the power and infinite potential of the human mind and brain that will free countless men, women, and children of their destructive habits, leaving them free to really enjoy living. Highly recommended."

—**Jacquie Forde, RGN, RM**, CEO of The Wellbeing
Alliance, a nonprofit Three Principles–based
well-being consultancy

"The principles Amy Johnson shares in this book straddle science and spirituality, and are revolutionizing how people approach behavioral change and the way they live their lives. If you're ready to change your habits for good, read this book!"

—**Michael Neill**, best-selling author of *The
Inside-Out Revolution*, and host of
Supercoach Radio

The Little Book of

BIG CHANGE

The No-Willpower Approach
to Breaking Any Habit

Amy Johnson, PhD

New Harbinger Publications, Inc.

Publisher's Note

This publication is designed to provide accurate and authoritative information in regard to the subject matter covered. It is sold with the understanding that the publisher is not engaged in rendering psychological, financial, legal, or other professional services. If expert assistance or counseling is needed, the services of a competent professional should be sought.

FSC
www.fsc.org
MIX
Paper from
responsible sources
FSC® C011935

RAINFOREST ALLIANCE CERTIFIED

If the only thing people learned was not to be afraid of their experience, that alone would change the world.

—Sydney Banks

Contents

Foreword
by Dr. Mark Howard

I am pleased to write the foreword to this book.

For the past thirty years, I have been helping clients to transcend their addictions, compulsive behaviors, and unwanted habits. Yes, human beings can live at levels that take them beyond addiction. They can do this when they understand the principles that reveal the spiritual nature of the human experience. When people have insight into these principles, they find a wisdom that guides them toward happiness, contentment, and well-being. This is the antidote to unwanted habits and addictions.

Thirty years ago, I was searching for a way to take my clients to a deeper sense of their well-being, to find a life beyond addictions. At the time, I was the director of an alcohol- and drug-treatment program at a major medical center. I was fortunate to hear a man named Sydney Banks speak about his spiritual understanding of life. He shared the principles of Universal Mind, Thought, and Consciousness, which shed light on the true source of our moment-to-moment experience of life.

During that presentation, I realized how emotions and feelings are created and how they are simply a reaction to the thinking I create through the power that stems from these spiritual principles. In that moment of insight, I realized that with this understanding, I could be happy—and so could my clients.

Gaining an understanding of these principles, which are presented in this book, gives people hope. It gave me hope: the hope that I could be happier and not be tied to habits or compulsive behavior.

Understanding the Three Principles

The three principles of universal mind, thought, and consciousness represent the spiritual nature of our human functioning. They are a formless energy that provides us the capacity to experience life.

Universal Mind is the intelligence, the formless energy, behind the universe. It is the energy that serves as the foundation for creation.

The hope for you: The understanding of mind gives you hope. You are a part of mind, and thus you have an innate intelligence that gives you the power to respond wisely and overcome unwanted habits.

Thought is the energy that allows for creation. What we create through the power of thought is all of our mental activity. Our opinions, memories, judgments, blame, excitement, and compassion are just a small sample of what we have the power to create in our minds.

The hope for you: Understanding the principle of thought as the power you have to create your own thinking is freeing. Your feelings and all of your experiences of life are the result of your thoughts about the circumstances of life, not a direct result of those circumstances. You discover you are not wedded to these thoughts; you have many different ways to look at your life.

Consciousness is the energy to be aware of what we have created through thought. Through the operation of consciousness, our thoughts are brought to life. The second we create a thought, consciousness brings the total experience of that thought to us. Our biochemistry, physiology, emotions, and behavior all follow our thinking. Thus, if you have a worry-filled thought, consciousness brings *all of you* to align with that thought.

The hope for you: The understanding of how thought and consciousness create such a real picture of your life will give you a new freedom. You will understand that you are not bound to that worry-filled thought that fills you in turn with pain and dread. This will allow you to easily find a perspective that is less reactive and more compassionate.

As your understanding of these principles deepens, you will demonstrate more of the human attributes that help you deal with your unwanted habits and compulsions. You will become forgiving, considerate, generous, appreciative, and loving. Through your insights into the three principles, you will find new, creative thinking that will help you deal well with the many life issues that come your way.

As my clients came to understand the three principles, they discovered that their habits or addictions were merely their way to try to feel better, to find well-being or peace of mind. And they realized that they already had within themselves the well-being they were searching for. They began to quite naturally realize the deep, positive feelings that already existed within their own consciousness, and this allowed them to end their attempts to find those feelings through the habit or the addiction.

They said they could now grasp that their cravings were just a result of a particular change in their thinking and that they could make the choice to not engage that kind of thought, thus ending their cravings. This is the power of understanding the principles. Once a person gains insight into these principles, he or she can avoid dysfunctional thinking and look for thoughts that are more helpful.

My clients' insights also helped in other areas of their lives. They discovered ways to improve their relationships with family and coworkers. Many of them described how they were living in deeper feelings of love and understanding.

Dr. Amy Johnson has brought the understanding of these principles to the field of habits and compulsive behavior. This is a new paradigm toward habit change. As she tells us repeatedly, the true process of habit change is not found in techniques and methods; it is found in the spiritual essence of our being. Not only do we have the potential to realize our true spiritual nature, but also, with that insight, we can transcend habits and compulsions. This is the power of her book—encouraging you to look toward the wisdom and well-being that is your true spiritual nature.

Amy lives the understanding that she is bringing to the readers of this book. She speaks from her own insights and gives readers the hope to overcome unwanted habits.

—Dr. Mark Howard
Three Principles Institute
Burlingame, CA
February 2015

Introduction

I wouldn't recommend asking people what they are *least satisfied* with in life. It's a downer question and won't do anyone any favors.

But if you *were* to ask, I bet you'd hear a lot about unwanted habits. As a life coach—even though I don't explicitly ask—I hear about people's areas of least satisfaction all the time, and I can attest to how often bad habits and old patterns enter the picture. Unwanted thoughts and behaviors are obstacles to what we want for ourselves. The most exciting dreams and the best of intentions can be quickly derailed when habits and repetitive actions take over.

And if having our dreams and intentions interfered with wasn't enough, many of us feel that we are powerless, mere victims of our habitual patterns. We know better, yet we don't *do* better, and we can't figure out why. Habits not only take us away from the life we want but also become ammunition we use against ourselves—proof that we should be better than we are.

Humans are designed to thrive; we have a natural bent toward it. Feeling good is our nature, and so we instinctively look to return there when we're not there. As a testament of our desire to feel good and thrive in life, we try everything we can think of—going to extreme lengths at times—to end our unwanted habits. That quest often ends in frustration and hopelessness.

It doesn't have to. When you view yourself and your habits in a new way, change happens much more easily than you have experienced in the past. The nineteen chapters in this book will help you see your habits in a way that renders them powerless and leaves you free to fully enjoy your life the way you are meant to.

A No-Willpower Approach

The book you're holding is quite different from other books you may have read about ending bad habits.

You aren't going to read about setting goals to be habit-free, using willpower to overcome your habit, or being more disciplined as a way to outsmart yourself.

This is not a book that urges you to examine your past, the overall state of your life, or the specific emotional voids that led you to your habit. You won't be asked to consider the external factors that trigger your habit, and you won't have to come up with a list of alternate behaviors to turn to when the urge to do your habit strikes.

This approach is different.

This book is based on the premise that your habit is an *impersonal, thought-based experience* that can be addressed without rehashing your past or analyzing your life. It is not about a lack of willpower or discipline, and it has nothing to do with being ignorant of triggers or not using the right coping mechanisms. *Instead, ending your habit is about deeply connecting with the truth of who you are and deeply seeing the true nature of your habit and yourself.* We will look at the intersection of spiritual and neuroscience principles to encourage those insights.

Your habit is rooted in an attempt to feel better, but that doesn't mean you have to radically change your life for your habit to go away. In very simplistic terms, nearly all habits start as a way to not feel what you're feeling, a way to leave the present moment—often by numbing out in some way—and return to a more peaceful, calm home base. Your habits are misguided attempts to feel

3

more comfortable in your own skin. And they are incredibly effective. They do take you out of your suffering for a short time. They quiet your painful thinking, transport you away from the moment you're in, and help you stay partially blind to your experience. When you're feeling restless, and you stumble upon some behavior, substance, or obsession that instantly soothes that restlessness, the habit has taken hold. From then on, the habitual thought or behavior looks like the best and fastest feel-better option available to you.

Your habit is also giving you valuable information about your state of mind. When you feel the tension and *dis-ease* that leads you to want to act out your habit, that dis-ease is your signal that you are lost in your personal thoughts, creating an uncomfortable experience for yourself with your own thinking. In that way, your habit is a helpful invitation to step back and let your mind clear so that you can reconnect with the truth of who you are.

So initially, your habit may be something you do to feel more like yourself in the face of some inner conflict or dissatisfaction. As your habit becomes more entrenched, however, *the habit itself* becomes the problem. Before you know it, the habit is a bigger problem than any pain it originally helped you to avoid.

Your habituated brain is now focused on keeping your habit alive, and it uses urges to do that. Urges are simply thoughts or feelings that encourage you to act on your habit. Urges can be anything, from a fleeting thought that says, *It's okay; just check your e-mail one last time*, to all-out warfare—something you feel throughout your body that hijacks your emotions, drives action, and feels near impossible to ignore, like a smoker's craving for a cigarette or an alcoholic's craving for a drink.

Soon, while your habit is still about avoiding your experience, the painful experience you are trying to avoid is the urge. Acting on your habit is still a means of distraction from your own inner experience, but the source of suffering changes.

That extremely uncomfortable drive to act on your habit is neurologically strengthened each time you obey the urge. The stronger and more frequent urges become, the harder it is to do anything other than give in to them, which sets in motion a painful, habit-reinforcing cycle. As you will see throughout this book, however, transcending your habit is always possible, regardless of the neurological state of your brain.

Habit is broadly defined in this book as *a repetitive thought or behavior that one wishes one did not experience*. I will focus on two types of habits: behavioral habits, such as gambling, being on the Internet too much, over-eating, overworking, overspending, or lashing out at your partner; and mental or thought-based habits, such as fears and phobias (fear of heights, public speaking, and so forth) or persistent thoughts (for example, thoughts about being judged by others, thoughts about something bad happening). Common fears and phobias are considered thought-based habits because the basis of the habit is *fear*, created by subjective, habitual *thoughts* that appear real and compelling.

When you think of a habit, you probably think of something similar to the behavioral habits mentioned above. In this book, however, persistent thoughts and mental habits are treated the same as behavioral habits, because *the basis for all habits is thought*. From moment to moment, we feel only what's on our mind—and it is how we feel, which is the direct result of thought, that drives 100 percent of our behavior.

The only difference between behavioral habits and mental habits is where the focus is. With behavioral habits, we tend to focus on the action itself. If you bite your fingernails, work to extremes, or compulsively clean your house, the outward behavior is what you call the problem. But despite this focus on behavior, it's thought that *underlies* the problem. The reason you do everything you do is because of how you relate to the thoughts that run through your head.

In mental habits, the focus tends to be more on your internal state than on overt behaviors. If you have habitual, insecure thoughts about your relationship, for example, the inner turmoil you experience as those thoughts arise feels like the primary source of your pain. Of course, you sometimes act on those thoughts, and your actions, no doubt, create even more pain, but the source of the problem *appears to be* your inner (mental) life rather than your outer (behavioral) life. Again, in reality, your inner, thinking life is always the direct source of everything you feel and everything you do.

The way I'm referring to *thought* here may be quite different from how you're accustomed to thinking about it. I'm not talking about the *content* of specific thoughts or about only conscious thought that you are aware of. I'm talking about thought much more broadly, as the creative force that allows us to experience and create life (Banks 1998; 2007). *All* human experience comes to us via the creative gift of thought. Without conscious *and* unconscious thought, we wouldn't have human experience as we know it.

Spiritual Insights That Can Change Your Habit

A spiritual understanding of life can lead to a fundamental, vertical leap in how you see the world.

The spiritual understanding I share in this book is derived from a field of spiritual psychology called the Three Principles, which reveals how our entire experience of life is created: the interplay of three universal principles describes the origin of all human experience.

The principle of *Universal Mind* describes the creative energy that is the source of all life. Universal mind is the power source of all living things—the universal, infinite intelligence that creates and powers our entire universe and everything within it. Universal mind is running through all of us, always. The principle of *Thought* is how we come to know or experience life. Everything we know comes to us via thought. The principle of thought is the vehicle that transforms the creative energy of universal mind into real life, manifest experience. And the principle of *Consciousness* is what allows us to experience what thought creates. Consciousness is like a movie projector in our minds—it brings thinking to life, delivering a vivid, sensory experience of what's actually taking place internally. Although our experience is generated from within us, it feels as if we are experiencing life as it is in the world around us. What is truly inside-out tends to appear very outside-in.

Taken together, the three principles of universal mind, thought, and consciousness account for every experience we ever have in life. Powered by universal mind, thought creates experience, and consciousness brings that experience to life for us. Every moment of our lives occurs *within* us by the interplay of these three principles. We are not the experiences we have—we are universal mind (spiritual energy) taken physical form. We have been blessed with the wonderful gifts of thought and consciousness that allow us the always-changing experience of life.

You are by nature full of peace of mind, clarity, and connection. By nature, you are confident, calm, and habit-free. You weren't born with your habit, and it is not an essential part of who you are. It may dominate your thoughts, emotions, and behaviors, but your habit says nothing at all about your basic nature—that part of you that is always there and always true, underneath your surface thoughts, emotions, and behaviors.

Because the core of you is thriving and habit-free—and it can't be any other way—you are never too far away from that truth. I know it may feel like you are light-years away from health and clarity. It did for me. But that's only how it looks when you are lost in thought. In truth, there is enormous momentum ready to lead you back to your innately healthy nature. Your resilience and your ability to reconnect with the truth of who you are cannot be stressed enough.

Your habits, as well as any personal thoughts, judgments, and insecurities you might identify with in life, are *thought*. We live in a sea of personal thought, so much so that we rarely recognize it as such. We take what floats through our minds as truth, assuming it reflects reality outside of ourselves. Actually, the reverse is true. Spiritual traditions throughout the ages, as well as modern physics, point to the fact that what we experience of the world around us is a reflection of our own personal thinking, not the other way around.

Think of it like this: You are a wise, spiritual being with infinite clarity and peace of mind. You are part of the greater intelligence that is responsible for all of life.

Beyond this, you are having a human experience. As a human being, you have a brilliant mind full of personal thought. Personal thought is yours and yours alone. It is the expression of the very human side of you, full of ideas about yourself and about life, full of opinions, judgments, fears, concerns, and preferences. The human part of you experiences thought, emotion, behavior, and the whole gamut of human experience. But because we so often lose sight of our healthy, spiritual nature, it is easy to get lost in that human experience and believe that's all there is.

We take our thinking very seriously, owning it as if it is ours and fearing it as if it can hurt us. In an attempt to feel more "like ourselves" and less uncomfortable, we try to fix or manipulate our experience. Ironically, when we resist or try to change what we're experiencing, we often reinforce it. The energy of resistance showers thought and emotion with attention, and so it dominates our experience even more. In contrast, when we accept our experience as it is because we deeply see that it is not us, it comes and goes, naturally and swiftly. We find ourselves with richer and more meaningful glimpses of the spiritual truth that is alive and well beneath our human experience.

It's as if we are the sky—always blue, always clear, with the sun always shining. That is our never-wavering spiritual essence. And our human experience is weather. Weather (thought, emotion, behavior) rolls in and covers up the blue sky at times. The storms can be so violent that they are all we can see; the clouds can be so thick that we forget the sun is there. But the weather doesn't disturb the sky. The sky *contains* the weather but is not affected by it, just like our spiritual nature contains our human experiences but is not affected by them. And the weather, like thought and emotion, is always temporary. Sometimes it comes and goes quickly. Other times, it lingers. Sometimes the weather is pleasant, and sometimes we curse it. But it is all surface-level and temporary.

What this means is this: There is a part of you that is totally and completely habit-free. When you are in the deeper emotions of peace, love, and gratitude, you are connected with your true self, and your habit is a non-issue. It is nonexistent.

When you are caught up in the human weather of your life—*thinking about* life rather than simply *being in* it—your habit crops up. It is associated with that part of you. Your habit is of the mind, not of the soul or spirit. It is not even of "you"; it is a creation of temporary, fleeting thought that comes and goes when left alone. Given that thought is self-correcting, your habit is also self-correcting, in a sense. There is a way in which you can let that experience float by—like clouds in the sky—without getting caught up in the storm.

You will read much more about this spiritual understanding in the pages that follow, because a deeper sense of these truths will make it far easier to dismiss the thoughts that encourage your habit. It is easy to become almost completely focused on the weather—your habits and circumstances—and lose sight of what you know to be true about yourself and your resilience. I will remind you of this throughout this book as a way of reconnecting you with what you already deeply know to be true.

Scientific Insights That Can Change Your Habit

Modern neuroscience has a great deal to contribute when it comes to seeing your habit in a more accurate and hopeful way. The brain science I will discuss in this book is the physical manifestation of the spiritual principles I've already introduced. In other words, the spiritual understanding points toward the nonphysical or the formless. In spiritual terms, thought is the vehicle that brings formless, spiritual energy into something we can directly experience. In scientific terms, a specific thought—or the action we often refer to as *thinking*—is the manifestation of spiritual energy that shows up in our physical body (in the brain).

In a neurological sense, you have your habit because of how you react to your own thoughts or urges. When you act on an urge, you strengthen the wiring of the habit in your brain. You may have heard the expression "neurons that fire together, wire together," which points to the fact that when two things occur together repeatedly—when an urge arises, and you then obey that urge—that leads to those events being even more strongly linked, neurologically (Shatz, quoted in Doidge, 2007). That means that each time you give in to an urge, you essentially strengthen the neural associations that represent the habit in your brain; you tell your brain to keep producing urges. Giving in to your urges can make your habit stronger and "stickier" over time.

I can hear you wondering (because I used to wonder the same thing), *How do I not give in to my urges, especially the horribly uncomfortable, hijacking ones?* Most likely, you obey your urges because giving in to them is the only way you know to make them go away. Given how terrible they can feel, it's no wonder your priority is for them to go away. Urges often come with enormous pressure—it feels as if the only way an urge will fade is if you obey it, thereby releasing the pressure. Even if you don't *consciously* make the decision to act out your habit, giving in and acting on your urge can begin to happen somewhat mindlessly, almost like a reflex.

The great news, which you'll see throughout this book, is that you actually don't have to give in to your urges to make them go away. You don't have to do *anything* to make those urges go away. They begin to go away on their own when you see the truth about them.

Brain research (Schwartz and Begley 2002) shows how the brain can change as a result of our own thinking, focus, and insightful understanding. Self-directed neuroplasticity describes the fact that the brain can *physically rewire itself* as a function of how we think about our own thinking. When patients with obsessive-compulsive disorder (OCD), for example, began to practice mindfulness—when they were taught to view their compulsive thoughts and urges from the detached standpoint of an observer, a standpoint that acknowledged that those thoughts *arise within* them but *are not* them—their compulsive thoughts and urges carried far less weight and were much easier to dismiss. Dismissing their urges meant they acted on them far less, which dramatically weakened the presence of those urges in the brain. This type of insightful, self-directed focus actually showed improvements in OCD symptoms that matched the improvements in patients who were taking powerful psychotropic drugs.

Jeffrey Schwartz's research with OCD patients is some of the pioneering work in this field, but the results have now been replicated in psychology labs around the world and on a wide variety of habits. At this point in time, neuroplasticity is a well-documented finding; the brain can change as a result of how we come to view and relate to our own thinking.

When you see your urges and drives for what they are—fleeting messages that do not represent "you" or signify your real needs or desires—they are stripped of their perceived power, and they become *much* easier to dismiss.

And when you dismiss those urges without acting on them repeatedly, the urges eventually go away. Without urges, and from a state of mind that allows you to rest in the truth about your essential nature, your habit is a thing of the past.

The Intersection of Spirit and Science

When you combine the *spiritual truth* that you are perfectly and completely mentally healthy and habit-free (*but for* your temporary, habitual thinking) with the *scientific finding* that your habit is made up of thoughts that fade on their own, your habit begins to look far less powerful and stable than it has.

When you consider the spiritual truth that thought (like all human experience) is forever ebbing and flowing, always being replaced with new experience, along with the scientific finding that the thoughts that support your habit (your urges) fade on their own when viewed in a deeper way, it becomes apparent how the only power this habit has is in your innocent misunderstanding of it. Although it feels fixed, unwavering, and unavoidable, it is actually fluctuating and changeable.

Habits are both spiritual and brain-based. The spiritual part is deep. It provides the basic foundational understanding—it is the part we can't see but can sense; we have a feel for it, an intuitive understanding of it. It feels like common sense, something we may not be able to easily explain but that we somehow *just know*. The science is the real-world manifestation of the spiritual. It is the data we can see, the understanding we take from the physical, observable evidence.

I don't want to give the impression that there is a dualism here. There is not. The spiritual truths are the truth of who we are and how the human experience operates at the most basic, fundamental level, *beyond and before the senses*. They point toward what we can't physically see, hear, or touch. They are the felt truth that comes *before* the scientific facts that we can sense directly. What we then observe in brain scans and in overt thoughts, emotions, and behaviors is the *physical manifestation of that spiritual realm*. In that way, it is after-the-fact.

The brain is a physical machine. The state of your physical brain is not fixed, and it cannot ultimately prevent well-being, happiness, or freedom from habits (which are all your default nature). In other words, the spiritual energy that is who you are—the energy that created and powers your physical brain and body— ensures that you can rise above the dictates of your brain.

The spiritual understanding is the often-missing piece of the puzzle; I hope this book will help you wake up to it. Looking at what comes *before* the already- manifest allows us to see the malleable, in-flux nature of life. You are not a fixed entity with a fixed habit—you are fresh in each moment, with infinite possibilities avail- able to you. As you continue to examine the spiritual and neurological perspectives together in this way—not as a dualism, but as the nonphysical and physical sides of the same coin—you will begin to see your habit and your own innate well-being in a very different way.

How My Habit Ended

I know the power in this approach firsthand.

I struggled with binge eating and bulimia off and on for eight years. Binge-eating disorder (BED) involves eating large quantities of food in a way that feels very out of control. People with bulimia follow those binges with some behavior to compensate for the calories just consumed, often by vomiting or using laxatives. I never vomited or used laxatives, but I did restrict my food intake and exercised in extreme amounts in the days following a binge. My compensatory behavior never fully cancelled out the sometimes thousands of calories I consumed in a binge, however, and my weight, moods, and overall peace of mind fluctuated wildly during those eight years.

It may sound strange to hear an eating disorder described as a habit, and I acknowledge that it is a somewhat controversial stance. But given the way habits are discussed in this book—as routine thoughts or behaviors that are impersonal issues and that exist only because we innocently act on the urges our brain sends out—the bingeing and purging behaviors that characterize BED and bulimia fit well within our treatment of habits. This book points toward thought as the underlying source of all habits (and the source of everything we experience in life, actually). It's not so much *what* we think—the content of our thoughts—but *that* we think, that is important. The whole of our behaviors, emotions, and experiences in life are thought-created.

Viewing addictions and disorders as thought-created habits is not only fair and accurate, in my view, but it is also incredibly hopeful. Our thoughts can change in a moment, and when they do, the behaviors that are based on them often change as well. When we are caught up in a habit, we are caught up in thoughts that appear real. Our fundamental nature hasn't changed—it can't. We are fundamentally well, peaceful, and mentally healthy individuals. But habitual surface thought can mask that wellness. When we mistake that surface thought for who we truly are, we suffer, and our habits look far more stable and serious than they are.

As far as habits go, I felt completely out of control when it came to BED and bulimia. I tried everything to end it. I am an unbelievably disciplined person, but discipline and willpower were never enough. In fact, the more I tried to get my binge eating under control myself by discipline or sheer force, the worse it became.

So I tried not *controlling* it but diverting attention away from it, distracting myself whenever an urge arose.

I tried preventing urges by avoiding the things I thought preceded a binge. I tried everything from traditional therapy to self-help to energy-based healing modalities. None of the things, which were supposed to help, ever worked.

I was "failing" at recovery, and I took it very personally. I thought there must be something I was missing, something I was overlooking, or something I was doing wrong. I felt like a supreme fraud when I worked with my own clients as a life coach. Who was I to help others when my life was so out of control?

When my habit was at its worst, I tried my best to lean on many of the spiritual principles that were already a part of my life. I viewed my mental dialogue as "passing thought" rather than "truth," and I knew that a vast majority of what ran through my mind each day was habitual, biased, and extremely quick to change, based on my own state of mind. I especially watched my emotions in that regard, knowing that if I was feeling anything other than peace of mind, that meant I was caught up in some personal thinking that did not reflect the wiser reality of life. These spiritual practices made a notably positive difference when it came to my habit, but I had a hard time fully embracing them because, in many ways, they clashed with what traditional psychology was telling me.

My therapists were wonderful people who were well respected in their field, but their approach of looking into the past, looking at my emotions, and examining triggers and other coping mechanisms wasn't helpful to me. They viewed my habit as a disorder or a mental illness, which naturally led them to view me as sick or lacking; their job was to try to solve or fix my problem. My spiritual beliefs, on the other hand, assumed that I was innately mentally well and always would be but that I had simply fallen into a habit of faulty thinking that appeared meaningful and real. My heart told me that my spiritual beliefs were the truth, but it was hard to argue with distinguished and well-meaning doctors who had been working with this issue for decades. I was torn, so I dabbled in both sides, always feeling somewhat conflicted.

Each of my therapists questioned whether I was secretly unhappy in my relationships, in my career, or with myself in some other way. They assumed unhappiness was what was driving me to act out in this way. Honestly, nothing could have been further from the truth. Sure, I was adjusting to the changes that came from setting up a life in a new city (I had recently finished graduate school and moved to Chicago), but so were many of my peers, and they didn't find themselves locked in a horrible binge-starve cycle. And sure, I was adjusting to life with my boyfriend-turned-fiancé-turned-husband, but our relationship was great. He was a source of strength far more than a source of stress. It simply didn't make sense that my life circumstances were to blame.

My therapists suggested I track the external factors that seemed to immediately precede or trigger a binge. Although there were some noticeable patterns to my binge behavior, there were also countless exceptions to every pattern. Yes, I *tended* to binge more on weekends than on weekdays, but I had binged on every day of the week at some point. I *tended* to binge more in the evening, but I could certainly recall morning binges as well. I *tended* to binge more around social events, but sometimes it was before the event, sometimes after the event, sometimes during the event, and sometimes I did not binge at those times at all. Chasing triggers felt like a game of whack-a-mole—as soon as I identified one trigger, a contradictory example would pop up. I now understand that external events do not trigger or cause binges—internal events (thoughts) are the sole cause of acting out a habit.

My therapists also suggested I make a list of activities I could do instead of binge eating, as if I decided to partake in this dreadful, obsessive habit because I was bored or didn't have other plans. I was told that I'd most likely have food issues my entire life, that they would probably peak when I was under stress, and that it would be something I'd always have to monitor. I can tell you today that nothing could be further from the truth.

Traditional therapy has helped many people, and in no way do I mean to criticize it across the board. I share the details of my therapy only because you may have also tried many of the things I was encouraged to try in hopes of ending your own habit. Tracking triggers, delving into the past, looking toward outside circumstance—these are the things many professionals believe are the solution to our problems, and it is true that some of these things are helpful at times. But the real solution is much simpler and much closer to home. The solution is not complex or hidden, and it is certainly not found in the past or outside of you. The solution to your problem is incredibly simple, and it lies within you, right now. As it turns out, I was much more on track with my spiritual practices than I could have known at the time. Therapy was helpful in many ways, but it did not help me end my habit, because it did not provide the insight I needed.

Then, one day, I found myself one step closer to that insight.

I came across a book called *Brain over Binge: Why I Was Bulimic, Why Conventional Therapy Didn't Work, and How I Recovered for Good*, by Kathryn Hansen. *Brain over Binge* is Kathryn's story of her own recovery from her binge-eating habit. She quit almost instantly—and permanently—after struggling with the habit for six years and trying everything imaginable to stop. The similarities between Kathryn's story and my own were astounding.

Kathryn was able to leave her habit behind so swiftly and dramatically because she came upon some information that gave her insight into her habit. When she saw her habit in this new way, continuing it was simply no longer a viable option.

The new information she stumbled upon came from a form of addiction recovery called Rational Recovery (Trimpey 1996). Rational Recovery differs from Alcoholics Anonymous in many ways, but primarily because it does not view addictions as diseases. Rather, it is based on an understanding of neuroscience and how habits and addictions are formed and sustained in our brain.

The approach *Brain over Binge* applies to binge eating, which can be applied to a huge range of habits, starts with the understanding that habits come from an evolutionarily old part of the brain called the *lower brain*.

The lower brain is responsible for the mostly automatic functions that keep us alive—our drives for food, water, sex, and anything else that ensures our survival. The lower brain is not rational, thoughtful, or intelligent. It is essentially a machine that regulates routine, which makes a lot of sense in light of habits. The lower brain grabs on to certain thought or behavioral patterns and fights to preserve them. The fact that the lower brain is focused both on survival and on developing and maintaining routine means that routine and survival are often intertwined and confused. The lower brain treats habits as if our survival depends on them, which explains why many habits and addictions feel like matters of life or death. Even when it is clear that your habit has nothing to do with survival, following through on the urge can *feel* absolutely essential.

When we don't realize how simple and often meaningless the lower brain's messages are, we innocently and understandably hear those messages as truth. The inner dialogue that tries to convince you to act on your urges reflects that misunderstanding.

All behavior begins with a thought. Our inner dialogue reflects that: *Who are you kidding? You'll never change! Just one more time; you can quit tomorrow.* These messages are nothing more than habitual, *temporary* thought consistent with the machinelike and unintelligent lower brain. The lower brain broadcasts these messages in a routine, unthinking way simply because it is conditioned to keep your habit alive—it is no more personal or meaningful than that.

In contrast to the lower brain, the higher brain is the conscious, decision-making part of your brain; it is the part of your brain that makes the decision to listen to the thoughts that tell you to act on your urges. The lower brain cannot control action alone, which means that the wiser part of you is actually in charge. It certainly doesn't feel that way, but when you see the truth of this, everything changes.

The simple neuroscience that I read about in *Brain over Binge* perfectly converged with the spiritual principles I had already been studying and applying to my own habit. The facts that "you" are not your thinking, that thinking is habitual and subjective and not necessarily reflective of the world around us, and that thoughts are always changing on their own, with no effort required by us, are the essential spiritual truths—now backed by modern brain science—that spelled the end of my habit.

I can't tell you exactly how I knew that my habit was over for good. All I can say is that I had a profound insight—or a series of them, more precisely—that led me to clearly see that my habit had absolutely no power over me. I saw that any power my binge-eating habit appeared to have (and it appeared to have *a lot* of power for most of those eight years) was power that I was giving it through the way I was thinking about it. I had been viewing my urges as a force that was larger than me, that had the ability to hijack me completely. When I saw that my urges were actually a temporary experience made of nothing but conditioned thought—and that I couldn't possibly act on that thought unless I chose to on some level—everything changed. My habit was soon over.

Although my habit was over quite quickly and effortlessly, I don't want it to sound as if I never had another thought about binge eating. I did. But as you'll see through the stories shared in this book, those later thoughts were night-and-day different from the strong, hijacking thoughts that had run my life in the heyday of my habit. They now had a different quality and were relatively easy to dismiss. They were not thoughts that felt like urges, because they lacked the emotion, physical symptoms, and urgency that characterized strong urges. My later thoughts about binge eating were less compelling and did not drive me to action.

Since my own fast and easy recovery, I've devoted half of my coaching practice to helping people end habits. Because I stopped binge eating by insightfully seeing some truths that go far beyond intellectual understanding, I can't promise to verbally explain *exactly* what helped me. If a set of behavioral practices or techniques had been responsible for my radical change, it would be easier to share exactly what was helpful. But the truth is, I had an insight into something that goes beyond rational explanation, and it changed everything.

So the ideas you'll read about in the chapters that follow are my best attempt to point you toward what I believe I saw, and what I see now, about how human beings operate. Stumbling upon the neuroscience related to habits in *Brain over Binge*, combined with my deep belief in the three principles that underlie all human experience, led to what felt like a serendipitous, magical merging of science and spirit that makes me excited to share it with my clients and, now, with you.

About This Book

The nineteen chapters that follow are new perspectives on the nature of your habit. Each can make a huge difference on its own, but studying all nineteen together will have the greatest impact. For that reason, I recommend that you read the chapters in the order in which they are presented. Later, when you're looking for additional insights or a refresher, feel free to flip through the book and read any chapter you feel drawn to.

This book is divided into three main parts: "Understanding Your Habit," "Ending Your Habit," and "Lifelong Change." "Understanding Your Habit" is twice as long as "Ending Your Habit," with good reason. As I've touched on already, ending your habit for good is far more about *understanding*—having a profound insight or new view of the nature of your habit—than it is about action. With insight, action naturally and effortlessly occurs. All of the chapters in this book, but especially those in "Understanding Your Habit," are designed to produce insight into your habit.

An insightful understanding is different from an intellectual understanding. When we have an intellectual understanding of something, we *conceptually* see how it works. It makes logical sense, and we can explain it to others. But an intellectual understanding does not necessarily translate into behavioral change.

With an insightful understanding, you hear something that touches you in a way that effortlessly produces change. It is possible to have insight with or without intellectual understanding. When something you hear reaches you on a deep level, and you don't *decide* to act differently as much as you simply *notice* yourself feeling and acting differently, that's insight.

The information in this book works by insight. If you're tempted to skip ahead to the chapters in "Ending Your Habit," please don't. The substance is actually in the deeper understanding and insight that begins to build from the earlier chapters.

This book goes beyond ending habits. At first, it may appear to be simply about what you do or what you think (your behavioral or thought habit), and that is fine. It may be preferable, actually. After all, you're here to end your habit, so first things first. But what I hope you begin to see is that the truths you'll learn about your habit—that it is based on nothing more than a single thought; that all thought is fleeting, temporary, and not inherently meaningful; and that your habit is represented in your brain but it is not reflective of "you"—are actually true of all of life. By the time you finish this book, you will not only be far closer to being habit-free, but I hope you will also have a greater sense of freedom and a deeper sense of purpose across the board.

You Really Want to Quit, Right?

To get the most out of the principles discussed in this book, it's important that you truly want to end your habit.

Some people aren't quite ready for change. The extreme workaholic who, although her habit is threatening her health, is ambivalent about giving it up—or the woman whose weekly shopping habit is something her husband wants her to give up but not something she views as a problem—may not necessarily find these insights as life-changing as someone who is clearly ready for change.

But if you do genuinely desire lasting and relatively easy change, you are in the right place. It's okay if you are scared or ambivalent about the process. It's even okay if you are skeptical or if you doubt your ability to change. As long as you truly *want* change and you take this information in with an open mind and an open heart, you're in an excellent position for these ideas to help you put an end to your habit forever.

And with that, let's dive in.

PART I

UNDERSTANDING

YOUR HABIT

1

Your Habit Is a Sign of Your Mental Health

When you feel bad, you'll do just about anything to feel better. The fact that practically everything you do is an attempt to feel good is an unmistakable sign of your inclination toward thriving. That inclination is present in all humans.

You are healthy, well, and peaceful by nature. This is why you describe the desire to feel better as "getting back to normal," "bouncing back," or "feeling like yourself again." Home base for all human beings—regardless of our present condition—is mentally healthy, content, and free of destructive habits.

The only thing in the way of that peace of mind is thought—whatever happens to be on your mind, floating across your mental screen, in any given moment. That moving, changing, vaporous thought can't touch your health and clarity. It only appears to obscure it at times, just as clouds can *mask* the sun, but they can't *affect* the sun.

When you don't know better, it can be easy to be caught up in the clouds of thought. When you are living from your head, unaware that wellness and freedom from your habit lie just beneath that temporary, habitual thought, it is easy to feel as if you've lost your way.

But rest assured, you've never truly lost your way. It's not possible. The very well and healthy part of you, which is completely untouched by your thoughts, habits, and behaviors, is always right there, fully intact.

You Are Always Doing the Best You Can

You are doing what appears to be your best option in each moment of your life. That doesn't mean you're always making healthy choices that ultimately serve you, but it does mean that you're doing your best given how you see things at any particular time.

Something within you desperately wants to feel better, but you don't always know how. That's where bad habits, destructive behaviors, and addictions come in. It's also where meditation, bubble baths, bike rides, speaking up, being quiet, taking a nap, eating ice cream, and any number of things people do in order to feel better show up. The options available to you are dependent upon your state of mind, so *anything* can be an attempt to feel better.

There is a popular saying in addiction recovery: your best thinking got you here. Everything you've ever done is the best you could have done in that moment, from the state of mind in which you found yourself.

You can't see what you can't see. If you don't see a better option—a better way to feel good—you're going to do what you can. If gambling is your thing, you might gamble. If working or performing obsessive-compulsive routines or shopping is your thing, that's what you'll do. People hurt themselves—they sometimes even kill themselves—in order to feel better, if that looks like the only option.

Looking back, I can see how many of the harmful actions I took looked like the way to go on some level; if they hadn't, I wouldn't have done them. Many years ago, when I was inhaling nicotine into my body, lighting the cigarette was what my best thinking led me to do.

Of course I knew it was harmful. I also thought it would be way too difficult, painful, and disruptive to quit, so I smoked. Although I knew smoking wasn't the best way to go in the big picture, the bulk of my thinking at that time led me to light up over and over—until it didn't anymore. When my thinking shifted, my best thinking led me to quit.

The habits you are here to break may look crazy to you and to everyone around you, but they have been the best way you could see to feel better when you needed it. Your best thinking got you here, and when your perspective changes, your behaviors will too.

Your Habit Is a Misunderstanding

Acting out destructive habits is not self-sabotage. You may intellectually know that your habit is harmful, and you may be thoroughly confused as to why it appears to have a hold on you. One thing I can tell you is that you're not doing it to sabotage yourself.

What often looks like self-sabotage is a misguided attempt at self-love. It's you doing the best you can in the moment to feel better, driven by love for yourself and a deep desire for wellness.

You're not doing it because you have low self-esteem or an "addictive personality." You're simply caught up in some habitual thinking that doesn't feel like fleeting thought. It feels much bigger and seems to suggest something about you as a person. It does not.

• • •

Todd was a client of mine who had a habit of meeting women online, having one-night stands with them, and then not wanting to see them again. Todd recalls that the first time he met a woman online and spent the night with her, he experienced "a rush." It felt exciting, taboo, and totally against how he was raised to think of relationships, which added to the rush of emotion he experienced.

As Todd acted out in this way more and more, he realized that the rush of emotions was fairly consistent. Before long, he had a quick and convenient way to feel better. He didn't consciously see it like this, but his habit became his go-to way to distract himself from painful thoughts and to feel better in a hurry.

Because he wasn't seeing it as clearly as I'm laying it out here (we rarely see our own habits plainly), Todd was confused by his habit. He couldn't deny the mental, emotional, and physical benefits he enjoyed in the moment, but he also felt incredibly guilty about his actions. He assumed he had some type of self-image problem—why else would he continually do something that left him feeling so low and guilt-ridden? He also wondered if this was another manifestation of his addictive personality. After all, he reasoned, he smoked pot in college. He also frequently used alcohol to relax. And now this. It looked like a far-reaching, very meaningful problem to Todd.

It's easy to see how Todd came to misunderstand the nature of his problem. He had heard talk of self-esteem issues, addictive personalities, and self-sabotage in popular psychology, on talk shows, in self-help books, and even in his university psychology courses.

But there was a far simpler explanation. With his first one-night stand, Todd stumbled upon a quick way to feel good. When he later turned to that behavior again, he wasn't sabotaging himself or trying to promote his own suffering; it was the best—albeit skewed and limited—way he saw to suffer *less*.

Your attempts at feeling good might look like staying in bed when you're depressed, using substances when you're addicted, or being unkind to others when you feel insecure. Those actions may actually produce more suffering in the long run, but that does not mean that your using them doesn't demonstrate resilience and striving for the wellness that is within you. When your state of mind shifts—as it inevitably will—you will see a better way of being.

Your habit is a useful indicator that you are in a low state of mind, using your amazing power of thought to your detriment rather than to your benefit. In those moments, all you have to do is step back and let your natural, peaceful state of mind take over.

Well-being is home base for all people. It's what we were all born into, and it is where we will always naturally strive to return.

2

Wisdom Will Show You the Way

It's obvious that there is an intelligence behind life.

We're powered by something bigger than ourselves. We all call it different names and think of it in unique ways, but nearly everyone—regardless of background, culture, religion (or lack of religion)—tends to agree that there is some beyond-human force that grows trees, spins planets, and turns embryos into chubby babies. Human action and intellect don't make those things happen.

And it makes sense that something that great and mysterious—something given such lofty labels as *spiritual energy*, *life force*, *universal mind*, *wisdom*, and God—would be unbelievably glorified. We don't feel worthy of it, despite the fact that we couldn't separate from it if we tried.

Because it is so magnificent, we expect it to look and feel magnificent. "If inner wisdom were working through me," we say, "I'd know it, and life would be blissful."

It seems like it would be a life-changing, lightning-bolt-from-the-sky type of experience. And very occasionally, it is. But more often than not, wisdom informs us in completely simple and ordinary ways, which we may not even take note of. It is ordinary, disguised as common sense more so than as a miracle. But common sense *is* kind of a miracle, isn't it? Isn't it pretty miraculous that we often "just know" the millions of little things we know in a given day? From where does that common sense come? We didn't have to learn it. We don't produce or create it. It's simply there for us to access.

Your True Nature

That formless intelligence that powers all of life *is* you, at your core. It is the health and wellness that is you, underneath your human thoughts, emotions, behaviors, and habits.

The immutable, fundamental nature of all living things is this love, wisdom, and well-being. You *are* clarity. You *are* peace of mind. You *are* habit-free, by design. Those things can't ever be changed or taken away from you.

Those things are your true, default nature, though that doesn't mean you always experience them. You often feel the exact opposite of peace of mind. You feel confusion and a lack of wisdom. I'm sure that you regularly experience yourself in your habit with no apparent sign of well-being, love, or wisdom around.

When you aren't feeling aligned with your true nature, you are experiencing your personal thinking. Thinking can be full of confusion and compulsion, but that confusion and compulsion can't touch your true nature. It is a fleeting human experience created by thought.

And as you now know, your habit is created by thought as well. The entirety of your habit is built upon, experienced, and maintained by the thoughts that arise within you, when you view them as truth.

Because your fundamental nature is habit-free and the presence of your habit means only that you have a lot on your mind, you will return to your natural, habit-free state when your personal thinking settles down. When your mind slows down and clears a bit—the way minds always eventually do—you return to your habit-free set point.

Think of your mind as a snow globe. The snow globe is self-correcting. When it's shaken, and snow is flying everywhere, if you want the snow to settle, all you do is stop shaking it. When you leave it alone, the snow settles on its own. Your mind is the same. When you stop getting involved in your thinking (by showering it with attention or emotion, by trying to deny or resist what's there, or by acting on your thoughts and thus giving them life), your mind settles down, and you reconnect with the peace and clarity that is always there.

Every person on earth reaches a calmer, wiser state when his or her thinking relaxes. Each time you find yourself feeling deeply peaceful, your personal thinking is taking a relative break. Each time you find yourself in the throes of anxiety or urges or general uneasiness, your thinking has revved back up.

Your thinking shifts from moment to moment throughout life. With more on your mind, your habit feels more compelling; with less on your mind, it is less so. That doesn't mean that people don't have habits for years; it just means that on a moment-to-moment basis, your habit looks more or less like something worth doing. The only determinant is how much is on your mind. The more you have on your mind, the more you live in a world of personal thought, ideas, opinions, and judgment. The less you have on your mind, the more you are innately connected with your true nature.

That may make it sound like there is a goal—to keep your thinking slow rather than revved up. But because your nature is a relatively calm, relatively slow mind, you don't have to make that happen. Your mind will calm down on its own at times—even more frequently when you are aware of your nature. Your only "job" is to see that it works this way. When you see that it works this way for all people, all of the time, you find yourself far more grateful for the highs and graceful with the lows. You find yourself waiting for your mind to settle down when it is shaken up rather than jumping in to fix it and unwittingly creating even more confusion.

Wisdom is always within you. It is there when your mind is calm, *and* it is there when you are lost in a lot of revved-up thinking. It's just that it is easier for you to feel the wisdom shining through when your mind is at ease.

Hearing Wisdom

The fast, frantic thought you have in the middle of an urge, or at any time in life, is a clear sign that you are not in a good state of mind for making decisions.

When you feel better and your thoughts are slower and more confident, you're in a position to trust a little more. What's in your head in a calm or relatively peaceful state of mind is far more trustworthy than what's in your head in an anxious or low state of mind.

Nicole began to navigate this by getting a deeper understanding of the nature of herself and her thinking. Nicole was a very impatient driver, to the point of experiencing road rage on a regular basis. She had a forty-five-minute commute to work each way in bumper-to-bumper Los Angeles traffic. Throughout most of her commute, Nicole could feel her blood pressure rising and her stress levels soaring. The stress she experienced to and from work affected her entire day—she arrived at work feeling aggravated and upset, which made her far less effective at her job and not particularly liked by her colleagues. Just as her mood was beginning to lift, it was time to drive home. Following the afternoon commute, she usually walked into her house to greet her boyfriend in the same bad mood she had felt at work. At some point, Nicole began having a glass or two of wine as soon as she walked in the door, so that she could unwind before her stress ruined her boyfriend's evening. The wine relaxed her, but she was concerned that it was the beginning of yet another unwanted habit that she would someday need to break.

When she became familiar with the spiritual principles in this book, Nicole began to see that her nature was full of wisdom. She could recognize moments in each and every day when her thinking naturally slowed down a bit and she found herself feeling nice. That nice feeling wasn't because of what Nicole was doing; it wasn't because she wasn't commuting or because she was doing something she enjoyed, although she did tend to feel peaceful at those times. The reason for her nice feeling was that in those moments her thinking wasn't full of frustrated, impatient thoughts. Her thinking wasn't as revved up, and she was able to experience more of the natural well-being and wisdom that lay beyond thought.

When Nicole was not experiencing a nice feeling—especially when she was in what she called "road-rage mode"—her thinking was very revved up. Her snow globe was shaken to the max. Rather than catching a glimpse of the intelligence of life within her, all she could experience was the brick wall of her own impatient thinking.

Just seeing this was immensely helpful for Nicole. She didn't have to do anything about or with it; she only had to see how her thoughts and emotions worked in this way. Nicole knew that her urges toward road rage—as well as the urges to unwind from her road rage with a couple glasses of wine—were signs that she was lost in highly charged, busy thought. Her actions were her best attempt at feeling better when she was in that state.

Because her nature was peace, her mind would return her there. She didn't have to make it happen any more than the snow globe has to *make* the snow settle down or the ocean has to *make* the surface waves calm down after a storm has passed. She was part of the broader nature of the universe, powered by the same incredible source that fuels every living thing, always fluctuating and changing. When her temporary, impatient thoughts slowed down, she'd be returned to a quieter place, where she could more clearly hear her own wisdom.

And hear her own wisdom she did. When the road rage wasn't part of her life, Nicole knew without question that her basic essence was free of habits and of road rage. Her wisdom showed up in myriad ways, pointing her toward the deeper truth about who she was. When I asked her to share with me some of the most notable things she had learned by looking within in those peaceful times, she smiled shyly.

"They are so *not* profound," she confessed, "but at the same time, they've sort of changed my life. It's like I get these nudges that feel so commonplace, almost like common sense. Like the other day, I was driving to work, starting to get a little irritated, and out of nowhere, it occurred to me to pop in an old CD I had in the car with music that I used to listen to in college. I never listen to that music these days, but you know, it took my mind off the traffic and helped me get into a really happy feeling. Walking into the office, I felt better than I had in months.

"And there have been a lot of times," she continued, "when a thought just pops into my head about the wine. I'll reach for a bottle and think, *Wine isn't the solution, a calmer mind is*, or I'll think back to one of our conversations, and it's like there is a space there, an opportunity to reconsider. In an instant, it's like I know I can dismiss that urge—like thought—if I want.

"Or I'll begin to react to a coworker in a way that matches my frustrated thinking, and it's like there's this split second when I see that I'm only acting on my state of mind. It's not the coworker or the situation; it's my own state of mind. Sometimes I can walk away instead, letting my thoughts clear before I say anything.

"These things sound so insignificant when I say them like this, but they make a gigantic difference. I really do see how wisdom is there for the taking. All I have to do is look within and listen."

We are all full of wisdom. It's who you are and what you are made of. It is always there for you, underneath the surface chaos of your habit.

When that surface chaos (made entirely of temporary thought that looks far more stable than it is) settles down, you'll be able to hear your wisdom. Listen for it. Look within and listen. It's not outside of you. Anything you hear from any professional—including me—can't hold a candle to your own wisdom.

The only thing this book aims to do is point you in the right direction—back toward the wisdom that is already within you, so that you can use it as a guide.

The more you begin to follow your own inner nudges and common sense, the further away from your chaotic, thought-based, surface-only habit you'll find yourself.

3

Why You Feel Hijacked

If you're anything like I was, you feel utterly powerless over your habit much of the time.

When the urge strikes—you know the urge, that feeling that the gravitational pull of the entire universe is yanking you toward your habit—it feels like it is only a matter of time until you give in.

But when you do give in to the urge, you don't do it willingly. It's not like you calmly say, *Okay, urge, you win again today*, in any kind of accepting way. You give in reluctantly—defeated, kicking and screaming, and probably with a whole lot of regret and anger and, finally, a flood of shame afterward.

Feeling powerless over your habit is far from pleasant, but there is something even worse. *You know better.*

You're smart, logical, and resourceful. More than that, you're wise. Something deep within you totally and completely knows that there is a better way to live. There are options, but you just can't see them. You know that quitting is absolutely possible, but as smart and resourceful as you are, you haven't quite discovered how to quit. Ending your habit may still look like something you learn to *do* rather than what happens when you come to *see* a different truth.

So there you are, feeling powerless and defeated when it comes to this crazy habit, all the while knowing that there is another way. You feel a massive pull to do your habit, but you also feel a massive pull to *not* do your habit.

You cycle from moments of empowerment (*I can and will kick this!*) to moments of disbelief (*What am I doing to myself? Why am I stuck in this?*) to moments of powerlessness (*I'm hopeless!*). You are caught up in back-and-forth thought.

My client Jackie felt that she needed constant reassurance from her boyfriend, Ryan. When an insecure thought floated through her mind, it set off an intense urge to gain comfort from Ryan. The way Jackie obeyed her urges was to immediately try to get Ryan to tell her how much he loved her or how committed he was to her. As you might guess, this behavior was not attractive to Ryan, and it created tension in their relationship.

Jackie's habit was especially frustrating because she knew better. She knew Ryan loved her, and she also knew that—aside from the problems created by her habit—their relationship was strong. When Jackie was feeling good, she saw her insecurities as unreasonable and unfounded. Yet when the urge to hear Ryan tell her he loved her struck, she felt completely hijacked by it. It was as if the need for reassurance was all she could experience. That feeling was so unpleasant that she acted on her urge time and again.

Sometimes you can consciously abstain from acting on your urges. You find a sudden burst of motivation, willpower, or focus; you fight the urge and win. Jackie sometimes experienced the urge to call or text Ryan and was able to distract herself or white-knuckle her way through it. When she had the wherewithal, she tried to remind herself that her behavior was hurting their relationship. Occasionally, that was enough to help her fight the urge; usually, it was not. Fighting, discipline, and willpower don't work often enough. If that were all it took, you'd already be habit-free.

So *why* do you keep giving in? Why did Jackie keep acting on her urges, despite the fact that it was hurting her relationship with Ryan and despite her intellectual knowledge that her insecurity was based on faulty logic?

We yield to urges because it's the only way we know to end the tension created by them. In that moment, giving in is all we can see.

Your Brain and Universal Mind

It often feels as if you are of two minds when it comes to your habit. In a sense, you are.

Your brain is an amazing machine. It is a physical machine that was created by and is powered by universal mind. Your brain is made up of many individual parts, each with its own unique functions. But let's simplify things and talk about the brain as made up of two parts: the lower brain and the higher brain.

Neurologically, your habit lives in your lower brain. The lower brain is the oldest, most primitive part of the brain. It is so old and so primitive that it is the kind of brain that is present in most reptiles and other not-so-sophisticated animals, which is why it is sometimes called the "reptilian brain" or—my favorite name for it— the "inner lizard."

The lower brain is habitual and unintelligent. It has no capacity for logic or any kind of higher reasoning. The lower brain takes note of and acts out patterns—it is a rudimentary pattern-producing machine.

The lower brain is also where the fight-or-flight response originates; it is responsible for maintaining basic biological functions and ensuring our survival. The lower brain generates the drive for food, water, and oxygen, as well as for anything else that it believes is essential to survive.

When you have a deeply ingrained habit, the lower brain acts as if your habit is *necessary for your survival.* Many of the habits we pick up are treated by the lower brain as if life depends on them. The lower brain therefore produces strong urges for the behavior, thought, or substance involved in your habit. Although Jackie knew better intellectually, when her lower brain was producing an urge for reassurance, it felt as if she'd die without it. Getting reassurance from Ryan was the only thing she could focus on. In that moment, it can feel like gambling, checking Facebook, or eating excessive quantities of food is necessary for your survival, despite the fact that they obviously aren't even beneficial behaviors. Remember, the lower brain doesn't use logic or reasoning—it simply acts out patterns and habits as if they were essential.

Similarly, when I was in the grip of an urge to binge on massive amounts of sugary foods, my brain was so hijacked that getting my fix was all I could think about. The lower brain's urges even appear to hijack the more intelligent portions of the brain, making logic and reasoning nearly impossible. There is little room for common sense when we are consumed with the lower brain's messages.

The urges not only seem necessary for survival, but they can also produce incredibly uncomfortable physical sensations. People often report that urges feel like tension. In some cases, the tension is minor enough that discipline or distraction can overcome it. In many cases, however, it is an enormous, mounting tension that you'd do just about anything to be rid of. Discipline and distraction don't have a chance against it. Obeying the urge and doing your habit is the only way you know to release that pressure.

Jackie felt stuck. Her habit of demanding reassurance from her boyfriend was habitual to her lower brain, so her lower brain acted as if her survival were dependent upon it and produced urges that drove her to act out the painful pattern. But because Jackie's true nature was health and wellness and she had a bent toward returning there, she was *also* driven to *alleviate* the incredibly uncomfortable urges from her lower brain. The only way she knew to alleviate them was to give in to them, which would temporarily release the pressure. Obeying the urges, of course, not only meant that she fell for her habit again and put more strain on her relationship, but also meant that—by repeatedly obeying the urge—she was actually *encouraging more* habit-related thoughts to show up. Jackie's lower-brain patterns were being reinforced every time she acted on them, and she couldn't see a way out of the cycle.

In order to feel hijacked, there has to be something for the lower brain to hijack. That something is the functioning of your higher brain.

The higher brain is more sophisticated and more advanced than the lower brain. It is intelligent, logical, and rational. It is the part where conscious decision making and voluntary motor behavior take place.

You would never in a million years voluntarily choose to act on urges if you saw another option. Up until now, you—via your wisdom and higher brain—haven't seen another option. But that is about to change.

Where the Hijacked Feeling Comes From

When an urge comes on, it often feels like "you" are being hijacked. The wiser, know-better, want-better part of you (your common sense or wisdom) is suddenly overwhelmed and incapacitated by your habit.

While your lower brain is producing urges for your habit that feel undeniable, your wisdom and higher brain are saying, *What are you thinking?* Battle ensues. The lower brain is fighting for its fix, emitting urges with emotional and physical symptoms to drive you straight into your habit. Meanwhile, the wiser higher brain is reminding you that you actually don't want it.

My wisdom would remind me that there was another way to see things. Jackie's wisdom reminded her that her behavior was irrational and that it was chasing Ryan away.

This is why it so often feels like "you" are being controlled by something that's not truly "you." The wise part of you doesn't want to keep living this way, but you are focused on the temporary functioning of the lower brain. "You" don't see a way out. You don't want to fall back into your habit, but your urges are so strong that you don't seem to have a choice in the matter.

Or do you?

The Lower Brain's Limitations and the Power of Wisdom

While your lower brain produces urges and behaves as if it is saving your life by sustaining your habit, it cannot actually act on the commands it doles out. Universal mind or wisdom—working through your higher brain (which controls your voluntary decisions and movements)—is where your actions ultimately originate.

You choose to act on the urges of the lower brain because it's the best way you see in the moment to feel better. You don't realize you have a choice.

Your thoughts can't make you light a cigarette or walk to the refrigerator. Jackie's thoughts couldn't send Ryan a text. Your voluntary behavior, operating via your higher brain, is required for those things. The lower brain can only broadcast messages to you, but because you don't know better, you convince yourself that if you do not act on your urges, all hell will break loose. Actually, the opposite is true. You choose what to do with those thoughts, based on what you understand about them and how they appear to you in the moment. It is a choice. It may not always feel like a choice, but ultimately, it is.

One of my spiritual teachers uses the metaphor of a backseat driver to illustrate our ability to dismiss thought.* Imagine you are driving your car and approach a red stoplight. And you've got someone in the backseat screaming, "Go! Run the light! Just do it!"—right in your ear. The screams are loud and annoying, but if you're the one behind the wheel, no amount of screaming can actually *make* you run the light. Habitual, lower-brain thought is the backseat screamer. Your wisdom and your higher brain functions are the driver.

When you begin to understand the origin and nature of those hijacked feelings, they are stripped of their perceived power.

You had control all along; you just didn't know that dismissing habitual thoughts was an option. In the following pages, you'll learn more about how it is not just an option—it's actually easier than you ever imagined.

The Brain Is Fascinating, but Don't Stop There

The brain is about as intricate and remarkable as any physical thing on earth. But there is another aspect of

---

* Thank you to Dicken Bettinger for this metaphor.

life that comes *before* the physical. It is the formless, spiritual energy that creates and powers everything that has ever been formed in the physical world—what I've been calling *universal mind*. This spiritual energy is not bound by limitations. It is unlimited, pure potential.

If your brain had a power cord, it would plug into this unlimited potential. Everything would plug into that source. That source is where everything was born and where everything eventually returns.

That spiritual energy is the one thing that never changes. While your brain and other organs evolve and age—and while *what* your brain produces (thought, feeling, sensory experience, urges) is always ebbing and flowing—the formless, spiritual energy that powers and creates all things is constant and unwavering.

It is packed full of creativity and promise. It can create *anything*. It has created *everything*. It accounts for the countless cases of miraculous healing that defy scientific explanation and for the times when we act outside the "dictates" of our brain.

It makes way for new ideas, new thoughts, and bursts of creative genius. It has given you every change of heart you've ever had, every hunch you've followed, and every dream you've pursued. It can give you a new understanding of life and your habit in an instant.

Those things come *through* your brain, but they aren't exactly *of* your brain—just as blood pumps through your heart and air passes through your lungs, but blood and air aren't *of* the heart or lungs. Million-dollar ideas and changes of heart become manifest through you but don't exactly come from you.

The brain is fascinating, but please don't stop there. There is a bigger, more profound, loving, and limitless place to look beyond the brain. Rather than stopping at the machine, let's look at what powers the machine.

Similarly, psychology is fascinating, but don't stop there. Every field of psychology focuses on what is already formed. Psychology focuses on the thoughts, feelings, or behaviors we see, all of which are in the past by the time we get around to analyzing them.

When we look beyond the fleeting, ever-changing form to the unchanging, stable energy behind it, we're focused on potential rather than problems.

It's so easy to focus on what is already formed, right in front of us, and get caught up in the details—the pesky habit, your troubled relationship, your anger problem, the fact that you don't believe in yourself enough. Those are the things humans grapple with.

They are the things we analyze in psychology. Unfortunately, analyzing those details doesn't always deliver the freedom we're looking for.

Transcending those details delivers that freedom. We transcend when we look at the constants in life rather than the momentary forms. We transcend when we look to the formless, to what makes it possible to even *have* brains and emotions and problems.

It is very much worth a look.

4

Your Habit Isn't Personal

I bet you've consumed enough popular psychology and self-help material about your habit that you could write your own book, if you wanted to. There is a ton of information out there about habits and addictions and how to best break them.

And yet there are reportedly 23.5 million Americans with drug or alcohol habits—and that's only Americans and only drugs and alcohol. That doesn't account for the millions of people outside the United States or the myriad other habits people have. Clearly, all of this knowledge isn't necessarily helping in any reliable, applicable, or widely generalizable way.

You can easily find volumes of information about how your habit started, how it is maintained, and how it can be stopped. There are countless books, articles, and blogs about the causes and the effects of your habit. Researchers talk about who has which habits and why some habits are more likely in some people than in others.

Nearly all of the current thinking about habits you'll come across puts *you* in the equation in a very meaningful way. Maybe you've been told that your habit is the result of something lacking in your life; I was told that. You may have heard there is something wrong with the way you view the world, handle your emotions, or relate to other people. Maybe you've been told that your habit hasn't gone away because you lack discipline, willpower, or the proper internal or external motivation.

At some point along the way, you've probably heard that you need to replace your old habit with a new habit or that you should meditate, rely on a higher power, make peace with your past, forgive someone you haven't forgiven, find more fulfilling hobbies, or love yourself more.

People everywhere are innocently—and *erroneously*—pointed back toward their own history, personality, or emotional state in search of a deeper understanding of their habit. But what if your habit has nothing to do with your personal history, psychological makeup, or the circumstances of your life?

What if the scenario is completely different—not only does your habit have nothing to do with what you lack, but also your urges provide information that's actually *helpful*?

It's Not About You

My client Christina had a shopping habit that was, in her words, "insane and out of control." It wasn't that Christina enjoyed shopping, the way many people do—she actually didn't enjoy shopping at all, despite the fact that she was constantly buying things. She felt driven to do it.

Christina grew up in a somewhat poor family with few material luxuries. Going to a store for anything other than a basic necessity was rare, and getting a new, optional treat happened twice a year: her birthday and Christmas. Christina had felt a sense of scarcity regarding material things for as long as she could remember.

When Christina graduated from college and started her first career, she could afford to buy things on her own for the first time. Her first few shopping trips were "exhilarating." She bought some basic pieces of furniture for her new apartment and a few new outfits to wear to her new job, and she put it all on her brand-new credit card. It was a rush unlike anything she had ever experienced.

At some point, however, it became obvious that Christina's habit was not about pleasure; it was something she did to avoid discomfort. She began to experience urges—times when she felt the overwhelming need to make a purchase—and she bought things as a way to release that urge rather than to bring herself joy. Christina's habit was taking over in other ways too. Her apartment was becoming too small for all of her possessions, and her credit card debt was adding up to the point that she was unable to make her minimum monthly payments. When Christina tried to simply stop shopping, she found it much more difficult than she expected. Despite the disappointment and shame that followed a shopping episode, she was unable to fight the urge. She felt hijacked by something beyond her control. It was as if making a purchase was the only way to stop the urge in its tracks.

Christina realized she couldn't stop on her own and sought the help of a therapist. When her therapist asked her how she felt when she shopped, Christina said she originally felt exhilaration, similar to the rush one might feel on a roller coaster. Lately, however, relief was her primary emotion—giving in to her shopping urge felt more like a much-needed momentary calm than anything else. Because buying new things gave Christina a sense of calm, her therapist suggested that she find other ways of feeling peace and calm in her daily life. Although this may seem logical, it was confusing to Christina, because she believed that she didn't have a preexisting lack of peace in her life that was remedied by shopping; it was the shopping habit that caused the lack of peace she felt. After all, nothing had been particularly lacking before this habit became part of her life. And her habit was not about the material things she bought, but about the strong drive to buy them.

Christina also talked a lot about her past in therapy, which took time away from discussing the problem as it was at the time. It's not that Christina's past was irrelevant to her habit, especially in the early days. It makes sense that the feelings of scarcity that marked Christina's childhood contributed to the exhilaration she felt when she first began shopping as an adult. But once the habit took hold, Christina's past quickly became irrelevant. She didn't need to resolve her past in order to become habit-free. Now that her habit was formed, what mattered most was that she could see her urges to shop in a new way. When she saw her innate health and her urges in a new way, she would be able to dismiss the urges and thereby put an end to her habit.

When Christina asked her therapist what she should do when those strong, hijacking urges came up, her doctor suggested that she do whatever it took to not give in to them. Her therapist knew that not acting on the urges would allow the habit to fade in time, but he had no idea just how mentally and physically consuming the urges were. This wasn't an issue of Christina not having enough discipline or willpower to stop; it was about her experiencing urges to shop that felt like a matter of survival, and obeying those urges because she didn't see another way. If it were as easy as "don't give in," Christina wouldn't have been in the mess she was in. In order to not give in, she needed to view her urges in a new way; otherwise, she was just white-knuckling through them.

Christina left therapy feeling weak, materialistic, and hopeless. Before therapy, she had felt that her life was quite good—the only "problem" was her habit. After therapy, she questioned that. The direction her therapy took suggested to her that she lacked character and that she was dissatisfied with her life. She now felt like a failure for not being able to fight the urge. Nothing could have been further from the truth.

Christina's therapist wasn't the problem. That was the current thinking in his field, and it was not as helpful as it could have been. A different, unbelievably helpful view is that habits aren't about your character or your circumstances. Habits are *thoughts* that feel compelling and often uncomfortable, but they are actually quite impersonal.

We all experience a steady stream of thought all day, every day. Those thoughts aren't *you*, they are simply life flowing through you. "You" are the space within which life unfolds.

All of that thought occurring within you comes and goes. It is in motion by nature. You innocently, unknowingly set your habit in motion with your thinking *about* your thinking and with what you believe about your urges. When you mistakenly view urges as dangerous, personal, unbearable, or somehow permanent, you naturally give in to them. Giving in looks like your best option for making the urges go away.

But as you begin to see that urges are simply passing thought—they aren't something to fight, and they certainly aren't an indication of your flaws as a human being—it becomes far easier to dismiss them. As you continue to see that you are healthy, well, and habit-free *by design*, it becomes far easier to rest in that understanding, without jumping on every thought that passes through you.

The *feeling* you get when you experience an urge is actually a helpful early warning sign; it's telling you to slow down and become suspicious of the way you are using your power of thought. Because we are always feeling our thinking—and urges are just one type of thinking—the tension you feel is simply a reflection of a busy mind. Your mind clears of thought naturally, on its own. The presence of your habit is an invitation to step back, wait, and let your mind slow down.

It has been said that humans are the only animals that speed up when they are lost. All other animals stop and wait to regain their bearings. We humans rush forward, pushing through with frantic, sped-up action. We think and do *more* when what is helpful is to think and do *less* so that we can be guided by something far wiser than our current thinking.

Your habit is nothing more than an innocent misunderstanding. It is not and never has been about your character; it is a valuable warning that you fear and act on when you innocently misunderstand it.

Your understanding is about to grow by leaps and bounds. Things are nowhere near as hopeless as they may feel.

5

You Need Insight,
Not Information

There are countless ways to know something and many varieties of knowing.

You're no doubt familiar with the type of knowing that is associated with your intellect. Who fought in the Eighty Years' War, the fact that Lima is in Peru, and how to fix a flat tire are fact-based or procedural types of intellectual knowledge. That type of knowing tends to feel relatively clear—you know that you know some things, and you know that you don't know others. Intellectual knowing is improved by studying, practicing, rehearsing, memorizing, and other *active* pursuits. You seek out information, and that information adds to the base of knowledge you can (usually) access when needed.

Knowing facts and understanding how things work is obviously important in many ways, but it is not without limits. Information is context dependent. Your ability to fix a flat tire isn't going to help when your house is on fire, and knowing that Lima is in Peru isn't going to help when you're lost in Africa.

A different type of knowing is insightful knowledge. What you know insightfully tends to feel quite different from what you know intellectually, because insight is a deeper sort of truth. The fact that you love your dog, that visiting your grandmother feels like the thing to do (and that accepting a particular job does not), or even that you prefer asparagus to green beans is insightful knowledge. You still know what you know—in fact, you probably know these things with more certainty and in a very different way than what you know about wars, cities, or car parts—but you'd be hard pressed to explain *how* you came to know them or *why* you feel the way you do.

While intellectual knowing comes about *actively*, through reading or rehearsing information, insightful knowledge comes about more *passively*, through—you guessed it—insight. There is nothing you have to do—nothing you even *can* do—to guarantee an insight. Insight often occurs when you are open-minded and you aren't thinking too much about anything in particular.

You do not need more information in order to end your habit for good. You have more than enough information already. In fact, all of the extraneous and misleading information you've heard about the nature of your habit may have made it *more difficult* to kick. What is needed to end your habit once and for all is insight.

Insight Changes Behavior; Intellectual Knowledge May Not

Adrienne was worried about her drinking. Her nightly wine habit had gone from one glass a few nights a week to two to three glasses every night, and when she tried to cut back on her own, she found it much harder than she expected. Although Adrienne could rationalize that a couple glasses of wine at night wasn't all that bad—she was still a functioning member of society, raising young children and doing exceedingly well in her career—it was starting to feel as if the wine had a hold on her, and she wanted to stop before it took over.

When we began coaching together, we talked about the things you read about in the first four chapters of this book. I shared with Adrienne that her wisdom would be there to guide her toward what was best for her, especially as she learned not to obey every urge she experienced. We talked about the fact that her habit was her best attempt to feel better and that she was doing the best she could from where she was in any given moment. And we talked about how fleeting and ultimately safe our thoughts and experiences are—even urges—when we're able to glimpse what is always true about us *beneath* our human experiences. I suggested to Adrienne that perhaps her habit was not personal in any way, and that suggestion was met with a huge sense of relief.

Adrienne's intellectual understanding grew by leaps and bounds. She could explain the lower and higher brain, and she saw that her fundamental nature was health and well-being and that urges—like all thought—would come and go if she didn't interfere. Like any quick learner, she picked up the concepts and information right away, but also like many people, she didn't have a deeper insight immediately. She got it intellectually, but not insightfully.

How can I be so sure she didn't see things at the level of deep, personal insight? Because her habit still *felt* like something that had control over her. The urge to pour another glass of wine was still something she saw no choice but to obey most of the time. Although Adrienne was definitely beginning to see her habit differently, her drinking showed us that there was room for Adrienne to "get it" in a more profound way.

Implications of Insight

Intellectual understanding gives you a fuller perspective on concepts, but it doesn't necessarily affect you personally. Insight, on the other hand, changes you from the inside out. When you have a deep, personal insight about something, you see a new truth that tends to naturally and effortlessly affect your behavior. In my book *Being Human* (2013), I recount a story from Byron Katie's book *I Need Your Love—Is That True?* (2006). Katie tells of how she was once hiking in the Mohave Desert and came upon a rattlesnake. She was instantly paralyzed with fear—images of someone finding her body weeks later flashed through her head. In her terror, something made her take a second look at the rattlesnake. When she did, she realized that the "snake" was actually a rope.

In that moment, Katie had an insight. A moment earlier, she had been positive that what she saw was a snake. Now, no matter what she told herself, she simply could not bring herself to be afraid of the rope. She saw the exact same object in a new way, and her thoughts, emotions, and behaviors radically changed as a result.

Although that story is a great example of how insight changes behavior, I don't want to leave you with the impression that insight is always that dramatic and impactful. Huge aha moments like Byron Katie's happen, but they are the exception rather than the rule. More often, insights are small and subtle. It's not just that you might not have a lightning-bolt-from-the-sky kind of experience; you might not even realize you had an insight at all until your behavior changes or life simply starts to feel different in some relatively subtle or indescribable way.

I had an insight about my own binge-eating habit— or maybe it was a string of insights, I really don't know— that made way for my old behavior to fall away quickly and relatively easily. I didn't learn and employ any steps to end my habit. It didn't feel active on my part (although that's not to say that I didn't consciously "do" some things). It was more that I saw my habit in a new light, and when I did, it didn't look like something I was powerless over, and so the behavior began to die out. Insight imparts the sense that "nothing changes, but everything is different." That's exactly how I felt—the only thing I had actively done was take in the teachings of my spiritual mentors and the information in *Brain over Binge* with an open mind and then follow my own internal inclinations about what to "do." Nothing much changed on the outside, but everything was different.

As my talks with Adrienne continued, things began to resonate with her beyond the level of intellect. Although we had talked many times about the fact that her urges were impersonal and somewhat predictable, she heard that message in a different way one day, a way that gave her a sense of distance from what was taking place in her mind. She began to view her lower brain as an urge-producing machine, and her urges felt far less meaningful and far less threatening than they ever had before. She saw something in a new way, and she suddenly felt different in relation to her urges, with little conscious effort or practice on her part.

Adrienne didn't instantly or completely stop drinking, but her drinking behavior did change. Most of all, it *felt* different. Adrienne enjoyed brand-new thoughts and was closer to change than she previously had been—by "seeing" rather than "doing." That's insight.

Bring On the Insights!

If you could force insight, you surely would have by now. Although there is nothing you can do to *produce* deep insight, there are a few conditions that encourage it.

The best thing you can do is give your intellect a break. Don't think too hard. When you hear a new idea or perspective on your habit—on *anything* in life—and you begin analyzing it, comparing and contrasting it with other things you've heard, you end up squarely in the realm of intellectual understanding. Your own biases and "this is like X, but unlike Y" thinking come into play and limit what you're able to see. You end up confirming or disconfirming what you already think rather than discovering something new.

Instead, see if you can let these and other new ideas wash over you with little judgment and evaluation. Read the rest of this book the way you'd read a novel or the way you'd watch a movie or listen to music—softly rather than firmly, loosely rather than rigidly. Read as if you're open to inspiration and insight rather than as if you'll be tested on this information later. With a less active mind, you're likely to hear things you wouldn't otherwise hear. The information will land in a deeper way.

As Adrienne continued to take in new information about her habit in an easy, non-analytical and nonjudgmental way, she saw things more and more deeply. Her intellectual understanding made way for deeper insight, and that deeper insight—which generally happened gradually, though there were some dramatic leaps—caused her wine habit to eventually come to an end. Adrienne didn't have to call on willpower or white-knuckle her way through any wine-free nights. Her habit died out on its own as she saw the truth about it more and more clearly.

When she had felt powerless over her habit, Adrienne could only see one version of reality. She was consumed by the hijacked feeling, and she couldn't possibly see things in a way that allowed her to make another choice than to obey her urges. It was never that those other truths didn't exist—it was only that she couldn't see them.

But as she gained deeper insight into the nature of life and the nature of her habit, she woke up to the truths that had always been there. Adrienne compared it to the feeling of waking up from a nightmare—when you're in the middle of a nightmare, you feel as if you are experiencing reality, but then you wake up and see a new reality. The moment you wake up, the nightmare is put into perspective, and it loses its power.

You can wake up to a new reality about your life and your habit. A deeper understanding of life is always possible, and it is always helpful.

6

Urges Are Your Inner Alarm Clock

Urges are thought. They create the physical, emotional, and mental pull toward the behaviors that make up your habit. As you now know, your urges provide helpful information, showing you that you are veering off course mentally and emotionally and that you are using your power of thought in a way that is not beneficial.

Your habit stays alive because you act on your urges. That is, if you didn't act on your urges, your habit would eventually go away.

Why do you act on your urges? We all act on urges because of how they feel and what we make of them.

Urges can be unbelievably uncomfortable. What you make of that mounting discomfort is that it is a force far bigger than you that is growing rather than waning.

Sometimes the only way you can see to end an urge is to give in and binge, or have another glass of wine, or text your boyfriend, or whatever your habit is.

Luckily, what you make of your urges—the way they appear to you—is based on innocent misunderstandings. The actual truth about them is very different.

A More Accurate View of Urges

In the most basic sense, an urge is nothing more than a thought. It may feel more physical and emotional than mental, but powerful emotions and strong physical sensations are the *outward manifestations* of temporary thought.

A thought about doing your habit pops into your mind, and when given attention, that thought snowballs. Before you know it, your mind is consumed by a parade of thoughts about your habit.

Urges are nothing more than thoughts. Those thoughts—brought to life by consciousness—can make your heart and your mind race. They make your vision narrow or your body tremble or your muscles contract and tighten. They might make you cry, squirm, or want to scream. And yet, they are meaningless and impersonal. They are passing experience—your brain putting on a show, doing what it can to keep your habit alive.

In neuroscience terms, you taught your brain to produce urges. The first few times you experienced an urge and obeyed it, you strengthened the connection in your brain between your habit and positive feelings. Your lower brain saw that when it produced an urge, you acted on it and felt good, which essentially told your brain, *This works! Keep those urges coming!* And so the urges continued. Each time you gave in to them, they became stronger than before, and your habit was reinforced.

In spiritual terms, your urges are a brilliant early warning system designed to alert you to the fact that you are using your power of thought against yourself. You are creating stress with your thoughts, and it's time to back off and let your mind restore itself to clarity.

Like an Alarm Clock

In many ways, urges are not much different from setting your alarm clock.

Your alarm clock is an unintelligent, nonthinking machine, like your lower brain. If you program it to go off at 6 a.m., it's going to go off at 6 a.m. Your alarm clock doesn't know that it's Saturday and that you forgot to turn it off. It doesn't know when you get a new job that allows you to sleep in until 6:30. It has no agenda or preferences. It doesn't care if you get out of bed, hit snooze, or rip its plug out of the wall and throw it across the room. Your alarm clock simply does what it is told to do; it lives out its programming until that programming changes.

Just like your alarm clock, urges are valuable information designed to *wake you up* to what's going on in your mind. If you are caught up in tension, worry, or unhelpful thinking, the unpleasant feelings that accompany urges are there to wake you up so that you can take a step back and let your mind restore itself, as minds naturally do.

Urges are the buzz of your inner alarm clock. Loud and sometimes startling? Yes. Harmful or dangerous? Nope. You don't take it personally when your alarm clock startles you awake in the morning. No matter how tired you are, you don't fear or get angry at the alarm clock; it is just doing what alarm clocks do.

What if you viewed your urges the same way?

Lara did, and it changed everything for her.

• • •

Lara lived in fear of her urges. She had what she referred to as a "major Internet habit." Lara's job required her to be at her computer for eight hours a day, and she was often glued to her laptop and smartphone when she wasn't at work. Most of her Internet time was spent reading about other people's lives, either on celebrity gossip blogs or on Facebook. She noticed that immersing herself in all of that gossip not only consumed huge quantities of time and took her away from her own job and hobbies but also left her feeling sad, lonely, and self-critical. She compared herself to the friends and strangers she snooped on, typically concluding that her life was lacking relative to theirs. Her habit dictated most of her day-to-day behavior and was robbing her of her freedom.

When Lara experienced the urge to disengage from life around her and surf the Net, she always gave in. She was terrified of her urges for that reason. Lara could not recall a single time when she had not yielded to the familiar drive to check up on her favorite friends or celebrities. To Lara, the urge and giving in to the urge were one in the same. It was as if she had no other choice.

When the thought of going online entered Lara's mind—as it often did—Lara panicked. But that one little thought—*Jump online! You deserve a break from work!* or *You won't be able to hold out all day; you might as well give in now!*—was completely harmless by itself. It was just a fleeting thought; an invitation to step back and be *less* in action, not more.

However, the way Lara reacted to and interacted with her urges gave *them* all the power. Lara met that innocent little thought with fear and panic, immediately jumping into *Why me? Why now? Why again?* She took her urges *very* seriously and *very* personally. She tried to reason with them, debate them, and problem-solve them. Her urges tripped off a chain of thoughts about all the reasons she would never change and how this habit might ruin her life.

Not surprisingly, the way Lara reacted to her initial urge thoughts fueled them, which led them to take on a life of their own. Before she knew it, she was in the throes of a full-blown physical and emotional urge experience that was extremely difficult to resist.

Lara's innocent, misguided response to her own urges created the very thing she most feared.

Turning Off the Alarm Clock

There were several things Lara didn't initially see about her urges.

For one, she missed the fact that her urges were not personal. She thought they were about her. She thought there was something lacking in her that led her to get wrapped up in gossip, but there never was. Lara was simply experiencing thought; the only problem she had was that she misunderstood and misinterpreted that thought.

Lara didn't see that the way she jumped on board the moment a thought about her urge surfaced was what led her thoughts to spiral into something much bigger. Before we began working together, she viewed that initial thought as a precursor of an inescapable Internet binge. She truly believed she was a powerless victim of her habit. Nothing could have been further from the truth.

As we talked more about how her habit began—how she had unintentionally taught her lower brain to produce urges by repeatedly acting on them in the past, as well as how she had come to mistakenly view her Internet time as the *source* of her peace of mind in those times—Lara began to experience a new perspective on her habit.

Rather than seeing her urges as a force of nature that was always lurking in the background, waiting for the perfect opportunity to strike—which felt very personal and instantly made her feel like a victim—she began to view her habit as an alarm clock. Her lower brain was just doing what it was taught. Universal mind—the spiritual energy that powers the physical brain—was sending her a wake-up call to step back and let her mind quiet down.

The presence of urges did not mean Lara had to act on them. Her Internet-gossip benders were not inevitable. Just as an alarm clock can't force you out of bed, her urges couldn't force her to spend hours online. Her internal alarm was sounding off only because that's what it was "set" to do, because it was part of a helpful warning system.

When Lara did give in to her urge thoughts, either by acting on them or even just by entertaining them and respecting them as truth in her mind, they got stronger. They would trigger other urge thoughts, and the combined effect would reach an emotional and physical tipping point that was difficult (but never impossible) to walk away from. When she didn't give in—when she began to notice the urge thoughts, simply view them as an alarm, and step back a bit to let her mind quiet down—they began to weaken.

Whether Lara was fueling her urges or dismissing them, they eventually faded. Nothing lasts forever. No thought, mood, physical sensation, or urge is ever permanent.

When Lara was able to view her urges as the programmed buzz of an alarm that she didn't have to answer, everything began to change. Her habit began to unravel.

The chain of events she once viewed as happening to her in a very intrusive and personal way no longer appeared that way. She was less wrapped up in those events. When she wasn't panicking and adding to the energy of an urge, she found that it began to fade, giving her relief from the need to obey it.

Your urges are no different from Lara's. She has no knowledge, special qualities, or extenuating circumstances that you don't have.

The urges you experience are only the routine signals your lower brain was taught to emit. They are no more personal than your alarm clock. If anything, they are your opportunity to step back and away from your habit rather than forward toward acting on it.

7

That Voice Is Not "You"

Jeremy was hearing voices.

He would be innocently going about his day, minding his own business, when they'd pipe up. Sometimes they would be very direct. *You don't have nearly enough money saved*, they might say. *Don't get too comfortable—you never know what could happen.* They would sometimes cut straight to the punch, convincing Jeremy that he was quite likely to end up poor and alone, sleeping under the viaduct.

Other times, the voices were understated. They could be sly and subtle, sneaking into Jeremy's consciousness without him even noticing, until his body was filled with an overwhelming feeling of dread.

Look how well your old college roommate Bill seems to be doing, the voices would say, implying that Jeremy was not where he should be in life. Or *Wow, that's a nice car Beth just bought,* goading Jeremy to compare and despair; or *The business next door just went through a round of layoffs,* suggesting that his job security was in question.

Jeremy was an exceptionally smart, down-to-earth, reasonable guy. Logically, he knew there was nothing to fear. He knew that even if he *did* lose his job or his savings, constant worry would only make things worse. From a relatively calm state of mind, Jeremy could see no good reason for his persistent worrying. It looked crazy and irrational, actually, when he looked at it objectively.

But when those fearful, homeless-under-the-viaduct fantasies came up, Jeremy often found himself frozen in terror; they felt so real and so compelling that they completely skewed his reasoning abilities. Within moments of the voices speaking up, what typically looked unlikely and a bit irrational began to feel like his inevitable future. Jeremy was hijacked by fear in the moment. Then, at some later point, he found himself "waking up" to see a calmer, more reasonable reality, as his mental slate cleared and the thoughts faded.

Jeremy was confused. The way he would flip from feeling calm and confident that he was okay to feeling scared and vulnerable—viewing the thoughts and voices as truth—scared him almost as much as the threat of being homeless under the viaduct. He came to coaching worried not only about his financial security but also about his mental health. How could it be that he was so taken over by these fears that looked absurd in the light of day?

"Just look at the thoughts that run through my head all day," he said. "I'm a basket case! One minute I feel great, and the next minute I'm convinced that I need to do something to ensure my safety. How do I know what's true and what's not?"

As we talked, one thing became clear: Jeremy assumed that the presence of those voices was meaningful. He had a lot of thinking *about* his thinking, which can quickly become confusing for anyone. Jeremy reasoned that because those fearful voices kept showing up in his head, they must mean something—if not about his financial state, then about his mental state.

I can certainly relate to that confusion. Can't you? We've all had racing, confusing thoughts—voices that repeat or contradict themselves—that we just couldn't make heads or tails of.

What Jeremy didn't realize—what most of us don't realize—is that the voices that threw him into a panic were not *him*. That was not *his* voice he was hearing. And it was not delivering a helpful warning. It was not saying anything trustworthy, meaningful, or true in any sense. It was simply thought about his habit, or what is sometimes referred to as the Addictive Voice (Trimpey 1996).**

Any Voice That Encourages Your Habit Is Not You

The Addictive Voice can be thought of as the voice in your head that represents your habit. In the case of behavioral habits, it is any line of thinking that tells you that following through on your habitual behavior or obeying your urge is a good idea. In the case of habits of thought, it is any habitual, painful thought pattern that, from a clearer state of mind, looks overblown or untrue. For Jeremy, his habit was the voice that convinced him that his financial security was in danger. That voice was the Addictive Voice.

** The term *Addictive Voice* is part of the Addictive Voice Recognition Technique (AVRT) as founded by Jack Trimpey within the Rational Recovery addiction treatment.

Our natural state is that of pure well-being and peace of mind. The only thing that can obscure that wellness is the thought patterns (often subjective and habitual) that we find ourselves regularly lost in. Considering this spiritual principle makes it much easier to distinguish the Addictive Voice from truth. Simply put, when a thought creates pain, it is not objective reality. A thought or inner voice that produces suffering is biased and untrue personal thinking.

The Addictive Voice is the voice that tells you you'll never be free of your habit, so why try? It loves to say things like *This one time doesn't count* or *You can start over tomorrow* or *If it hasn't worked before, why would it work now?*

In Jeremy's case, it was the voice that warned, *Don't relax; you're not safe. It could all end in a moment, and you could be out on the streets.* Jeremy's Addictive Voice urged him to squirrel away as much money as possible, and chastised him for spending money. It also warned him to take its warnings seriously. *You might think you can dismiss me as irrational fear, but you'll be sorry.*

It's easy to see how one could become as confused as Jeremy was. Each time he began to see clearly and realize that his fears were unlikely to materialize, the voice would try to convince him that he was putting himself at risk when he was *not* worried. Jeremy was living with a steady stream of conflicting messages.

One of the most important things you can come to see about your Addictive Voice—about any thought that encourages your habit or derails your efforts to change—is that this voice is only fleeting thought; it is not "you."

In chapter 3 we talked about feeling hijacked, as if you are of two minds. It's as if "you" are momentarily flooded by a steady stream of temporary, changeable thinking.

"You" are always there. You can't and don't go anywhere. But your basic, healthy nature is sometimes obscured by loads of personal thought. The Addictive Voice is part of that thought. To revisit the weather analogy I described in the introduction, the Addictive Voice and all of that personal thought is what darkens the sky—clouds and storms—and your healthy, habit-free nature is the clear sky. Weather comes through and sometimes causes a disturbance, but it is always self-correcting. It comes and goes on its own, and no matter how severe it is, it never affects the sky in any lasting way.

The more you see that "you" are not your painful thoughts, urges, or the Addictive Voice—that "you" are not anything that feels confused or conflicted or harmful—it becomes much easier not to take the Addictive Voice seriously.

You are the awareness that notices the Addictive Voice. You are the witness to it, the consciousness that *experiences* urges and inner conflict but *is not* urges or inner conflict.

And the Addictive Voice is not something you have to believe. It's the *Addictive* Voice, not *your* voice. Ultimately, despite how gripping it feels, it is nothing more than fleeting, temporary thought that floats through your mind.

In Jeremy's case, he knew he was going to be okay, just as he knew that worrying had absolutely no positive or protective function. Jeremy's only problem was a simple misunderstanding: he took the fearful voices seriously, assuming that since they had been there and so adamant for so long, there must be a nugget of truth in them. They must reflect "him" in some way, he reasoned.

Because Jeremy took the thoughts and voices seriously on some level, they affected him. But viewing them as meaningful and important was the *only* way they could possibly hurt him.

Freedom

The more Jeremy learned about his Addictive Voice and about thought in general, the more freedom he experienced.

As Jeremy gained a deeper grounding in the truth that thought comes and goes and is not necessarily something that needs to be respected, believed, or acted on, it became much easier for him to let the voices argue while he himself sat back and simply observed.

He began to identify much more with the awareness—the consciousness—that was witnessing his thoughts than with the thoughts themselves. As he insightfully saw that Addictive Voice messages were only fleeting ones that reflected his habit-inflicted brain's "opinions," but not *his* opinions, they lost their power and were much easier to discount.

And once these thoughts were discounted, they didn't come around quite as much. They didn't go away completely, but they certainly decreased in frequency and changed in intensity. Most important, Jeremy's reaction to and relationship with them changed.

Because Jeremy began to view his Addictive Voice as harmless, it didn't really matter if it was yelling or not. Sure, he may have preferred it to be completely quiet.

But he was ultimately able to transcend those thoughts when he noticed them.

Jeremy began to see *all* mental confusion as a clear indication that he was lost in thought. If clarity was his nature, confusion must be temporary thought. When he found himself gripped with fear, his mind racing with ideas about how to secure his income and save more money, he took a mental step backward and began to witness the fear, without falling into it. Although the fear was still present, he knew better.

From this perspective, the fear no longer overwhelmed him the way it used to. Jeremy viewed it as the Addictive Voice—only his habit at play—and that made it much easier to dismiss.

Today, when Jeremy's financial fears rush to the surface, they simply don't impact him in the same way. "You wouldn't believe it," he confided in our last coaching session. "I almost *like* when those fears come up now. It's sort of funny to see how dramatic and urgent they sound, now that I know that they are nothing more than old, unhelpful, habitual thought. In a strange way, they make me feel really grateful—they show me how far I've come."

Turning what was once a source of pain and confusion into something that sparks gratitude and good feelings may sound extreme, but it's entirely possible. If Jeremy can do it, you can too.

8

All Thought Is Temporary and Fleeting

Your entire life is made up of one fleeting experience after another.

Some experiences feel clearly apart from you. You experience a thunderstorm, the flu, or a mosquito bite, and those things are obviously not "you"; they are only what happens around, within, or to you. Other experiences feel more internal; the line between them and you seems less clear. The thoughts that run through your mind, the emotions you feel, and the urges you dismiss or obey are experiences you are having as well. They are no more "you" than a thunderstorm or mosquito bite, although they can *feel* like "you," because they appear to occur within you. Still, "you" are the witness to all that you experience, inside and out.

Everything you experience is temporary. You are not it, it is not you, and none of it lasts very long. It is fleeting; by the time you notice it, it is already changing.

This steady stream of experience that makes up your life is like a river. New thoughts, emotions, and other experiences are always flowing toward you and then away. The source of the river is something beyond the psychological, human realm. The nonphysical, spiritual side of life is the *source* of our physical, human experiences.

Water splashes onto the banks of the river at times, but water that comes to shore always returns back to the river. There is a constant ebb and flow, coming from the source and returning to the source. The nature of the river, beneath any surface waves, is calm and clear. The nature of you, beneath any surface waves (thought, emotion, other experience), is also calm and clear, with unending peace of mind and clarity.

Thought Is Everything, and Everything Is Thought

Although we bear an extremely wide variety of experiences, they all stem from thought.

Everything you experience—from what you feel and see to what you hear and taste—comes to you via your own thinking. In other words, your thinking determines what you experience in each and every moment. You will see that this is true if you look at how personal and subjective our experiences are. No two people see the same movie, hear the same song, or react to any circumstance in life exactly the same way. We experience everything through our own thinking, and then our thinking creates a picture of life that we assume reflects objective reality.

To see this truth in action, notice how your experience changes when your thinking has changed. When you're sitting around the dinner table and your sister tells a detailed story about a vengeful waiter spitting in a patron's meal, the next bite you take suddenly isn't as delicious. The food didn't change, but your thinking created a different experience of it.

Or imagine you're engrossed in a movie, just beginning to tear up as the lovable hero lies dying, and a cell phone rings behind you. Your thinking immediately shifts. You are reminded that it is only a movie, and the emotion you were feeling so strongly isn't the same.

We don't directly experience any kind of external "reality"; rather, we take in sensory information from the world around us and our own internal kaleidoscope uses it to create a picture that we then call "the way life is." This is how it is that every person who ever walked the earth has his or her own unique version of reality.

The dreams we have at night provide an excellent metaphor for how our daytime thoughts work. When you dream, it is clear that you are experiencing nothing but your own inner world—an inner world that does not match the outer, physical world. Your mind is projecting a series of images and experiences that appear to you—in your dream state—as reality, while, in the physical world, you are soundly sleeping in your bed.

You feel fear, joy, or confusion in your dreams. You see colors and vivid, lifelike images, just as you do in your waking life. You might even wake up with a racing heart, sweating, your legs kicking at imaginary bad guys. It all appears real until you wake up and realize it was just a dream. In that moment, you see that it was entirely created by thought, and the lingering emotions then fade.

Your waking life is created by thought in the same way. Because you're awake rather than asleep, and because we live in an elaborate world of form centered around the physical things in our environment, it always appears as if your experience is the direct result of the world around you.

But although it will usually appear as if your co-worker's rude comment is what made you upset—or falling into your habit again is what made you frustrated—your feelings are never a direct result of what is happening in the outside world. It can't possibly work that way. What is true is that you are always thinking, and that as you think, you *feel your thinking.* Your own steady stream of thought is the only thing you ever directly experience.

You can't feel your coworker's comment, your habit, or your surroundings directly. You can only feel your thinking about those things. This also means that nothing outside of yourself "makes" you do anything. Triggers don't make you fall into your habit. Stressful circumstances don't make your habit come to the surface. The only thing that can ever make you do your habit is acting on the urge (the thought) to do your habit. The only thing that determines your habitual behaviors is the way you relate to the thoughts that pass through your mind.

Isn't this excellent news? Because nothing outside of you can make you do your habit, there is nothing out there you have to change or avoid. The only change that has to occur for your habit to become a thing of the past is a change in perspective—an insight.

New Thought

Because the river of thought is always flowing and experience is ever changing, new thought is possible in any moment. Your entire experience can radically change with a single new thought.

We can't necessarily control our thinking any more than we can control the flow of a river, but we don't need to. When we see that old thought is constantly being washed away, replaced with new thought, we only have to wait, and our experience will change.

Thought simply is. It's not good, bad, harmful, or helpful; it's not personal, and it's not "yours." It is just thought. Given that you don't produce your own thought (it shows up in your head from who knows where), and given that you can't control it, you can't exactly claim ownership of it, can you?

All sorts of thoughts run through your mind all the time, and those thoughts create your experience in any given moment. But there is nothing to manage or change. It is all temporary. You don't have to take it so seriously, because "you" aren't creating it. It's not "your" thought, it's simply *thought*. You can take it or leave it. Even if you choose to leave it, there is nothing you have to do. It will leave you.

Logjams

Although the nature of thought is that it is impermanent and impersonal, always moving and changing, we certainly don't always experience it that way.

Smart, thinking adults tend to create logjams in that river of thought. We ruminate. We feel stuck. And especially in the case of habits, we live out the same experiences over and over. We are unknowingly, unintentionally creating our experiences of stuckness when we stand in the way of our evolving experience, and we stand in the way when we think about our thinking.

As I discuss in my book *Being Human* (2013), children are an excellent example of how thought naturally flows. Children experience thought just like adults do, but they don't think *about* their thinking—their thoughts come and go naturally, unimpeded. I watch my children (who are three and five years old) naturally and swiftly cycle in and out of thought all day long. My son gets upset and throws a temper tantrum; within a few minutes, however, it's completely over, and he's singing to himself as he plays happily. My daughter tells her brother that she never wants to play with him again, only to be completely past whatever upset her just moments later, when she's looking around the house for him.

Children bounce back so quickly because they don't think about their thinking. They don't judge their tantrums (despite the fact that the adults around them do), so they simply feel what they feel and move on. They don't have expectations for themselves of being consistent or having stable, unchanging moods, and so when they aren't stable and consistent, it's not a problem. And because it's not a problem, those moods come and go easily, without issue.

Thought arises within us, and we pay it little attention or we pay it a lot of attention. You pay virtually no attention to hundreds of thousands of thoughts you have every day—*What time is it?* or *I like her shirt* or *Time to let the dog outside*—and they simply come into your awareness and then leave your awareness, with no elaboration. When they leave, they make way for new thoughts.

Thoughts like *Did he just give me a dirty look?* or *I want a cigarette* can be met with no fanfare at all, or they can be elaborated on, repeated, respected, and even acted on.

When you look at it this way, doesn't it seem somewhat arbitrary that we grab on to some thoughts and make them our truth and that we simply let others go, almost unnoticed?

The difference between a person for whom a particular thought or behavior is a habit and the person for whom it is not is that the person with the habit entertains, takes seriously, and ultimately acts on some thoughts that others do not. That's it.

Chapter 3 described the case of Jackie, who needed constant reassurance from her boyfriend. Like Jackie, you may wonder how your partner feels toward you at times. When those thoughts floated through Jackie's mind, she didn't see them as passing thought—she saw them as truth. She showered them with attention and acted on them often, making them even stronger. But most likely, when those thoughts float through your head, you let them go. The way you view and interact with those thoughts determines how they affect you and determines whether you end up with a habit like Jackie's.

The difference between what happened when Lara (chapter 6) heard the thought *Fire up the Internet! See what gossip is out there!* and what would happen to you or me if we heard that thought is in the thinking about the thinking. It's in the attention given that thought and the extent to which it is taken seriously.

The simple thought *You could eat the whole thing!* felt compelling, emotional, and gripping when I was binge eating. It came with pressure and felt like something I *had* to act on. It is now completely different. The emotion and pressure are gone. A thought is just a thought—we can act on it or not, and either way, it will eventually fade and be replaced with new thought. Jackie, Lara, and I are no longer gripped by our old habits, and because of what we see about the subjective and fleeting nature of thought, we are unlikely to be gripped by them in the future.

What This Means for Your Habit

As you see the truth about thought, you naturally begin to hold it less tightly. Your habit is—and always has been—nothing more than a series of temporary, fleeting thoughts, no matter how valid, stable, and worthy of action they look.

When you let the river of experience flow, it flows quite naturally. That doesn't mean you never hit currents or run into rocks. You will still unintentionally create logjams—that's what humans do. But the more deeply you see how our experience operates, the fewer logjams you find yourself in.

At some point, you see through your habit. You begin to realize that it is only thought-created experience occurring within you. You can witness it without diving into it. You can experience it without being hurt by it.

And then it starts to unravel.

9

Willpower Is the Wrong Tool

People do break habits by using discipline and willpower. But it is not easy.

Willpower requires resources. You need to feel relatively good. You need energy and focus that you can call on for support. When your energy is depleted—perhaps because you're tired, hungry, sad, or in the middle of an urge—willpower is not always possible.

Luckily, there is an easier way.

• • •

Your habit is alive because you have an urge that feels worthy of action. The more consistently you act on urges, the stronger and more frequent they tend to become. You also become more accustomed to acting on your urges rather than stepping back and letting them fade.

The antidote to acting on your urges is seeing the truth about them. Despite the emotional and physical punch they might pack, they are a temporary experience. They are harmless in and of themselves. They don't require action. You can have the experience of an urge and do nothing; it will fade.

You weren't born doing your habit. Your habit isn't natural to you; it is artificial, innocently created by you as a function of the way you relate to and act on your thoughts. When you look at it this way, it's clear that thinking is what formed your habit and thinking is what maintains your habit.

Your habit is the manifestation of your relationship with the thoughts that float through your mind. The way you view, relate to, and act on thought is the sole "problem." Your habit is just the consequence.

What Is Willpower?

Willpower is more thinking. Willpower is after-the-fact thinking that attempts to trump your original thinking.

Employing willpower is an attempt to think your way out of a problem that is thought-created to begin with. If that sounds like a big mess, you're right—it is. When you rely on willpower, you are piling on more thinking when *less* thinking is exactly what you need.

Let's imagine that you're trying to eat in a healthier way, but you have a doughnut "habit." Your doughnut habit—like all habits—is thought-created. The reason you eat so many doughnuts, even though you also desire to eat better, is because you have thoughts (urges) that suggest you eat doughnuts. When you find yourself with the thought I *really want a doughnut right now*, you take that thought as truth. It sounds compelling, meaningful, and somewhat stable. Waiting for the doughnut thought to fade away or passing up the doughnut for a healthier option either doesn't occur to you or it feels too unpleasant to actually try.

If you were to use willpower to deny your doughnut urges, you would notice your A *doughnut sounds really good right now* thought and then proceed to layer new thought on top of it in an effort to squash it: *Yeah, but you'll regret it later!* or *No, you will not eat that doughnut! You are stronger than a doughnut! You can do it!*

The most critical flaw in the willpower approach is that thoughts aren't necessarily crushed by new thoughts falling on top of them. Actually, just the opposite is more likely to occur—those thoughts you are trying to dispel become *stronger* when they are showered with attention and met with resistance. Volumes of neuroscience research show us that what we focus on is mentally activated and strengthened. Attention paid to a thought about doughnuts, for example, increases the neural firing that produced that thought to begin with. (This is essentially the flip side of the research on which this book is partially based, which shows that when we *dismiss* a thought or urge—thereby removing our attention from it—the neural firing that produces that thought or urge decreases.)

Research conducted on thought suppression shows us this as well. When research subjects were asked to *not* think about something (white bears, for instance), guess what? Their minds were flooded with thoughts of white bears. The instruction to *not* think about white bears sets into motion a search for all fleeting thoughts of white bears so that one can prevent or end such thoughts. Scientists called this the Ironic Monitoring Process because—quite ironically—the quest to *not* think about something, by its very nature, produces *more* thoughts about it (Wegner 1989).

Arguing with or trying to suppress your original doughnut thoughts puts a whole lot of attention on that innocent little circle of deep-fried dough. And more attention doesn't make it go away—it actually makes it stick around.

A second problem with the willpower approach is that trying to overpower unwanted thoughts or cover them with new thoughts treats thought as though it were harmful and dangerous in and of itself. As you have seen many times in this book thus far, it is not. Thought itself can never hurt you; only *what you make of thought* can.

In time, any thought you happen to be experiencing will fade on its own. If you look back, you'll see that you've never once gotten permanently stuck in a thought or emotion. All human experience is temporary.

If thought is temporary and self-correcting to begin with, it doesn't make much sense to chase thought away or to try to reason with it using *more* thought. That would be a little like trying to change the weather. No matter what kind of weather you're getting, it will eventually change. No matter how harsh the winter is, spring always comes, every year. There is not only nothing you *have to* do to make that happen, but there's also nothing you *can* do. Just like you can't change the weather, you can't necessarily change your thoughts or emotions on a dime. Sometimes you can play a part, of course, but overall, efforts to manipulate your human experience often backfire.

Using willpower or motivation to try to overpower unwanted thoughts or urges implicitly imbues the original thoughts with power they don't actually have. *There is nothing to overpower, because there is no inherent power there to begin with.* If anything, urges alert you to the fact that you are getting caught up in your thinking. Luckily, that is a fully self-correcting "problem."

It would be infinitely simpler to begin to see your doughnut thoughts for what they are—habitual, temporary experience that is not *you* or *yours*—and allow that insight to render those thoughts powerless. Robbed of their source of power, they will fade on their own.

A third flaw in the willpower approach is that because willpower requires so much energy and focus, your ability to use it is inconsistent. Think about the effort it takes to refocus on a new thought when your mind is hijacked by an urge. Even when it works, it works only in that very moment. You might be able to ignore one particular doughnut thought, but you've used up a lot of your own mental and emotional energy to do so, and you've showered your doughnut thoughts with attention in the process. Now you are left mentally and emotionally drained, and you've increased the potential for more thinking about doughnuts in the future. That doesn't bode well for your ability to use willpower on your next urge.

The fact that willpower requires effort means it will fall short at times. When you are not at your physical, mental, or emotional best, willpower is harder to muster. Those are times when your higher brain (required for willpower) is somewhat compromised and your lower brain is leading the charge. Ironically, when you most need willpower, it is least likely to be available to you.

When we're talking about applying a steady stream of willpower and discipline, perhaps the most important question you can ask—even more important than "Does it work?"—is "What is it that I ultimately want?"

You want to be habit-free, of course, but at what cost? Isn't freedom what you ultimately want? Freedom from the obsession, freedom from urges—freedom to use your mind and body in a way that feels healthy and helpful and that allows you to enjoy your life to the fullest—isn't that what you really want?

If it is, consider that more fighting isn't the answer. More fighting is not supporting your quest for freedom, because you want freedom from the fight too.

Freedom comes from seeing a new truth.

Leaving Willpower Behind

To say that Valerie was worried about her children would be the understatement of the century.

Valerie spent inordinate amounts of time mentally playing out scenarios that involved her children becoming sick, being rejected by their friends, having freak accidents, and enduring practically any kind of suffering imaginable. None of these things were actually happening or had actually happened. There was no real-world indication that Valerie's kids' lives were likely to look anything like the images her mind created. These worries were simply thoughts that floated into Valerie's mind on a regular basis.

As is often the case when we're hijacked by a thought, part of Valerie (her innate wisdom) knew better. The habit-riddled part of her (her current thinking) didn't care about that. It was going to worry whether the worries were reasonable or not.

Because that wiser part of Valerie knew better, she took action to change things for herself. She understandably turned to willpower, because that was what she thought was helpful. The idea that her worry-filled thoughts were something she didn't have to change or fix never occurred to her, as it never occurs to many of us.

So, onward with willpower Valerie went. When she found herself paralyzed with fear by her disaster-filled thoughts, she stepped to the plate with everything she had to be the voice of reason, to motivate herself away from her painful thoughts, and to fight back.

You don't have to think this, Valerie! she'd tell herself, trying to speak louder than her fears. *The kids are fine— look at them. There is no problem right now.* But telling herself those things when she was already in a fearful state of mind—already low on resources and already far down the worry path—was rarely effective.

Look at the evidence, she'd tell herself, trying to use logic to overpower her fear. At other times, this might have helped, but when her mind was hijacked by crippling fear, logic felt irrelevant.

Innocently, Valerie worked hard to will her way into peace of mind, to no avail. Worry is exhausting enough. Trying to motivate yourself out of worry is grueling, and all of that focus on the fear only kept it alive in Valerie's awareness.

Finally, Valerie saw another way. Through our work together, she began to see her fears as nothing more than meaningless and habitual human experience. There was something incredibly freeing about realizing that the horrible imagined scenarios about her children were not personal or meaningful. There was no message in them for her, and there was nothing she had to do about them. They were simply passing thought, nothing more. They weren't even "hers" in any real way. They were simply unwanted, familiar thought that often visited and thus came to be expected. The more she thought they would show up, the more they did.

Valerie learned that she could use those worries as a warning signal that her imagination was having its way with her. Then she could become aware of how she was using her power of thought before it went further. Valerie gradually felt more and more free to do nothing with her fears, which freed up a whole lot of time and energy. Ironically, she found that the less she did with or about her fearful thoughts, the more they left her alone. They retreated more quickly—and on their own—and their visits became less frequent.

Within a few months, Valerie reported that her fears had decreased to the point that she couldn't remember the last time she had been truly gripped with worry about something happening to her children. Fearful thoughts still floated into her mind at times—they were a well-worn habit, after all. But the less Valerie made of their presence, the less she experienced their presence, and soon, the less presence they had—all because

Valerie set willpower aside and gave up trying to chase her thoughts away.

When Valerie saw her fear as passing, powerless thought, she no longer needed the will to overpower anything.

10

All Thoughts Fade

As you know quite well by now, urges are habitual, emotional thought. They are habitual, at least in part, because they've been acted on, reinforced, and given much attention and importance in the past. For that reason, the lower brain gets a lot of mileage out of urges. But there is one problem (from the inner lizard's perspective): as soon as you deeply see the truth about urges, they lose their power, because their "power" was an illusion. Urges never had any real power at all.

The Inner Lizard

In chapter 3, I talked about the differences between the lower brain and the higher brain.

The lower brain—also called the *reptilian brain* or the *inner lizard* because of its presence in the earliest, most primitive reptiles—is rudimentary and machine-like. It is like your inner alarm clock, unthinkingly carrying out its habitual patterns. The lower brain picks up on patterns and habits and fights to keep your habits alive, partially because it believes they are essential for your survival. ("You" may have a stake in keeping your habits alive too, because they help you temporarily feel better.)

But although the lower brain is certainly skilled at *producing* urges, it is not capable of *acting* on them. Decision making and complex muscle movements require the more sophisticated abilities of the higher brain. That means that no matter how strong an urge might be—no matter how insistent the inner lizard may sound and no matter how many urges it might toss your way—your lower brain alone is completely powerless to enforce it. You have wisdom that you can learn to call on in any moment, regardless of what your brain is doing.

Remember the metaphor of the person screaming at you from the backseat of your car, which I shared in chapter 3? If you are behind the wheel, no matter how loud someone screams at you to run the light, that person can't *make* you do it. You may feel bullied and powerless, but that's only your perception of the scenario. You have control the entire time. Whether to run the light or not is your choice to make. Your lower brain is in the backseat. "You"—your wisdom and your higher brain—are the driver.

When I was leaving my binge-eating habit behind, I liked to imagine my inner lizard at work. I imagined a scaly green lizard with no arms or legs; he had a gigantic megaphone (I'm not sure how he held the megaphone up to his mouth with no arms, but the details aren't important). My inner lizard was *loud*. He produced urges that felt hijacking—urges that narrowed my vision, made me hyperventilate, and consumed my attention such that the only thing I could focus on was finding food. It seemed that he was nearly always talking to me, saying things like *You know you're going to binge today, so you might as well just do it now,* and *You need a break from life… A binge would be a great escape.* Sometimes his commands were more impatient and to the point: *Go to the store! Finish it!* When he wasn't verbally taunting me,

I simply felt overcome with the physical drive to eat (although I could usually sense some wisdom in the background, reminding me that eating wasn't what I truly wanted to do).

I imagined my inner lizard bouncing around while he ranted and raved, but with no arms or legs, he had no real mobility. He was all bark and no bite. He literally had no ability to *do* anything about any of his commands and threats.

The same is true of your inner lizard.

Choice

Before you're aware that the inner lizard can only produce commands and can't possibly act on them, the commands feel compelling and ominous. You feel powerless over those thoughts because you believe they will eventually win out. They seem louder and stronger than you are.

But that is an interesting statement, isn't it? "*They* seem louder and stronger than *you* are." *They* are not *you*. You are experiencing them, so you are not them. There are two separate, independent entities: you and the urges.

When you insightfully see that the only way an urge will be acted on is if you (via your own wisdom and your higher brain) *choose* to act on it, things begin to turn around. It's not that the urges immediately go away. And it's not that they are instantly painless. You may still experience them. It's just that you begin to see them in a new light. Perhaps you see an armless, legless lizard with a megaphone, like I did. A part of *you* sees the source of those urges in a new way. You see the thought and the inner lizard as the loud but powerless forces of nature they are.

Your higher brain is completely responsible for all of your voluntary movements. Just as the backseat driver can't apply your foot to the gas, your lower brain can't make you act on your habit. Even when your habit is a mental one—like Jackie's habit of needing reassurance from her boyfriend, Jeremy's financial panic, or Valerie's fears about something happening to her children—you can hear the inner lizard's screams and see them for what they are: all talk. You come to see them as loud but powerless, empty threats. They are your imagination run wild.

While we don't necessarily have any input into the thoughts or commands that appear in our awareness, we do have a say in whether we obey them. Neuroscientists refer to the ability to veto any thought that occurs to us as *free won't*. The presence of urges (or *any* thoughts, for that matter) is not our business—our free will cannot determine what shows up. But the choice to *respect* or *act on* those urges is where we do have some say. We have free won't.

No matter how loud and powerful your urges are, *you* (via wisdom and your higher brain) make the behavioral choice. It may not feel like you have a choice at times, especially if you haven't yet fully seen that you are in charge. But the choice is always possible.

The Lizard Turns Hoarse

Knowing that there is no thought or urge in the world that can make you do anything is a game changer, isn't it? The inner lizard's threats and commands are harmless. And it gets even better—they are also temporary.

The less attention you pay the inner lizard, the faster it loses its voice. In that sense, that armless, legless lizard with a megaphone is a lot like a stray cat. The more you feed it (by respecting what it says, obeying it, and trying to reason with it), the more it comes around. The more you see that there is no point in paying much attention to it—because it is powerless and fleeting—the less it comes around.

The more you dismiss your urges, the faster they fade. And just to make sure you don't put any pressure on yourself, even if you *don't* dismiss your urges, they will *still* fade. Everything fades and changes eventually. No single experience is permanent.

Remembering who you really are underneath your habit makes it much easier to allow urges, thoughts, and emotions to exist without being so personally affected by them. As I've said many times in this book thus far, *you* are not your urges, thoughts, or emotions. Those are experiences that occur within you. They are things you observe or witness, but they are not you.

You are the awareness that is able to witness them. You are that healthy, clear, habit-free space within which urges and every other human experience occur.

Settle into yourself—the *you* that watches your urges come and go—and let the experience of your urges be there. The experience is a temporary one; it is already on its way out by the time you notice it.

Watch your lizard throw a fit. Listen to it scream commands at you. And simply wait for it to lose its voice.

It eventually will.

11

When You Don't Give In to Urges, Your Habit Changes

Mario once had overwhelming urges to play online poker. In the year prior to our working together, he gambled away nearly $45,000.

The only thing keeping Mario's gambling habit alive was the fact that he saw his urges in a way that led him to repeatedly act on them. The urges themselves weren't the problem. Urges have no inherent power—they are the armless, legless inner lizard, the backseat driver who's screaming at you to run the red light.

If Mario had deeply seen that his urges were powerless, he would have never gambled as much as he did.

Rather than see their powerlessness, he, like most of us, focused on their strengths—the rush of energy, the tension that built up within him, the panic he felt, and the intense drive to get his fix. Mario would have done just about anything to reduce that tension and begin to feel better. For a long time, the only way he knew to do that was to obey the urge and gamble.

Each time Mario obeyed an urge, he strengthened the neural circuitry that supported his habit. Acting on his urges essentially told his lower brain to keep the urges coming, and the more Mario obeyed his urges, the more his lower brain kept them coming.

The Shift

When Mario began insightfully seeing his urges as temporary thought that would eventually fade on its own—no matter how strong it felt—he began to feel as if he had a choice.

With that choice, he stopped giving in to the urges as much. He still *experienced* urges to visit his favorite casinos or poker websites, and sometimes he would follow through. But other times, he would wait them out, and when he did, they always faded.

When Mario stopped acting on his urges as often, one of the first things he noticed was that the urges changed a little. They were still there, but it didn't feel like they were hijacking his mind the way it'd felt before. He felt less consumed by them—suddenly there was more distance between him and the urges.

Mario's urges became less and less intense and less and less frequent, until they were no longer an issue. At some point, his urges stopped entirely. With no more urges for Mario to potentially act on, there was no more habit, and Mario's gambling problem was over. That doesn't mean he won't experience urges in the future. It's just that, as his understanding shifted, his experience shifted.

At some point, when you stop acting on urges and you no longer give them attention, they stop showing up. When and how that looks is different for everyone. The important thing to know is that the more you see your urges as harmless, fleeting thought, the easier it becomes to not act on them. The less you act on them, the weaker they become and the less you experience them.

It's worth noting that if Mario had stopped acting on his urges to gamble by discipline or willpower alone— without having seen a deeper truth about himself as innately healthy and habit-free, and without having seen a deeper truth about the nature of thought—there's an excellent chance that he would have taken up a different habit in future times of stress. We all know people who swap habits in that way. Because they don't see the deeper truths this book is pointing you toward, they white-knuckle their way through the end of one habit only to later pick up a new one.

The understanding that nice, peaceful feelings are accessible to you whenever your thinking settles down makes it such that you are unlikely to swap habits. Your current habit has nothing to do with the specific thoughts or overt behaviors you have—it is about using a behavior to relieve your internally generated discomfort (that is, mere thought) rather than stepping back and letting your self-correcting mind right itself naturally.

Your Plastic Brain

The brain is an incredibly efficient organ. The lower brain fights to keep patterns and habits in place once they are formed. This is why habits take hold relatively quickly. Once your habit is met with a rush of neurochemicals and reinforced by you obeying its urges, there is momentum in favor of keeping that habit alive.

But that doesn't mean the momentum can't shift.

You are spiritual energy (universal mind). That trumps physical organs and neural circuitry. Because the source of all life is pure, unlimited potential, your brain does not impact your ability to experience deep peace and well-being. That All-That-Is energy makes anything possible. So shifts in awareness and understanding are always possible.

Shifts are always possible in neuroscience terms too. In the introduction, I briefly discussed the concept of self-directed neuroplasticity, which refers to the fact that the actions of the *mind*—how you think and where you focus your attention—can physically change the *brain*. (Sharon Begley's 2007 book *Train Your Mind, Change Your Brain* offers an excellent presentation of this fascinating research.)

Scientists have found that the brain is far more malleable, or "plastic"—hence the term *neuroplasticity*—than had previously been thought. A dramatic example of this is the fact that the brain changes to compensate for losses in other areas; when someone has had a stroke, for instance, the unaffected brain areas begin to pick up the slack. The brain displays this same plasticity on a much more mundane level as well—consciously deciding to focus on something in particular (or to *not* focus on something, as in the case when you choose to dismiss an urge) changes the neural makeup of the brain.

This means that as you decide to *not* act on an urge, the momentum shifts in your brain, and it is poised for change. Jeffrey Schwartz and Sharon Begley's (2002) work with patients with obsessive-compulsive disorder (OCD) used brain scans to show that a self-directed shift in attention that resulted in patients *not* obeying their urges resulted in a weakened presence of those urges in the brain. The neural structure of the section of the brain where patients' OCD was represented was physically different. With time, those patients with OCD experienced fewer and fewer urges and compulsions, and the intensity of those urges lessened, until there was nothing left to obey. With nothing left to obey, their habits failed to impact their lives.

When there are no urges, the only thing that can cause you to do the thing that was once your habit is your own free will. You could do it if you deliberately chose to. But then it would no longer be a habit. When you are no longer acting on urges, your habit is essentially nonexistent.

It is worth repeating that *how* this happens is personal and unique. It looks a little different for everyone. Some people have a moment of insight that instantly changes things for them, but it's more common for a new understanding of your habit to unfold gradually. For me and for many of the clients I've worked with, the insights were quite sudden, but the behavior took some time to catch up. I saw in an instant that my urges to binge were not me and that I did not have to give in to them, but the behaviors associated with my habit died out more gradually. There was a period of time when I did occasionally give in. It felt different, however—I was no longer hijacked, I was aware that I was making a choice, and my binges were far less intense than they had been.

Every person's experience is different, but one thing is the same for us all: if you begin to see your urges as powerless and stop giving in to them, they will begin to change. With no power given them, there is no neurological energy to maintain them. How, when, and the amount of time that takes is different for everyone.

Although we don't have scans of Mario's brain to look for physical evidence of change, we don't really need it. Mario certainly doesn't need it. He knows that when he began viewing his urges to gamble as powerless thoughts—nothing he needed to respect, fear, or act on—he stopped acting on them as much. When he stopped acting on his urges to gamble, his urges changed. They were weaker and less frequent and became easier than ever to dismiss.

Today, nearly eighteen months after my initial work with Mario, he reports that his urges are completely gone. Although the thought of gambling occasionally crosses his mind, those thoughts don't pack the same punch they once did. They not only *are* powerless, fleeting thought, but they also now *feel like* powerless, fleeting thought. Mario hasn't experienced a strong urge to gamble in several months.

Again, this doesn't mean Mario won't experience urges in the future. He could at any time. But because Mario views his urges in a new way, he is quite unlikely to act on any future urges. He now knows to take a step back and let any urges come and go, and his insightful understanding makes that far easier than it once was.

PART II

ENDING YOUR

HABIT

12

Wake Up to the Soundtrack of Your Mind

Your lower brain (inner lizard) can be quite persistent. That's part of what makes it so confusing and difficult to dismiss.

Think about it—it tells you virtually the exact same things over and over in a voice that sounds like your own. *Of course* you begin to identify with those thoughts! Even when you intellectually know better, the lower brain's repetition and persistence—full of empty promises to help you avoid the hard parts of life and feel better in the moment—are pretty persuasive. It makes sense that it would become difficult to distinguish your habit-laden thoughts from what *you* truly want.

Luckily, the consistency of those habit-encouraging thoughts makes them easy to identify. When you recognize them for what they are, you're more likely to see them as thought, rather than truth or reality, and you're less likely to get sucked into acting on them.

And when you can experience them without getting drawn in, you are free.

Inner Lizard Thoughts Are Consistent

Your habit-reinforcing thoughts are predictable. They are like a playlist of favorite songs set on repeat. They call to you with the same emotional pleas time and again.

In her book *Steering by Starlight*, Martha Beck (2008) talks about how the inner lizard has predictable stories that you can easily spot, which helps tremendously in viewing them as "neurological junk" that is safe to dismiss (Hansen 2011). Beck encourages readers to make a list of their inner lizard's "favorite tunes." The more quickly you can recognize particular messages as coming from the lower brain, the less likely you'll confuse them with "you" or take them seriously, and they will be much easier to dismiss.

Makes sense, doesn't it? Want to try it? Which habit-encouraging tunes does your inner lizard have on its playlist? Here are some examples from some of the people you've read about in this book:

- Regarding her nightly wine habit, Adrienne (chapter 5) usually heard some variation of this from her lower brain: *What's the big deal?* That message came in different words and contexts, but the same basic theme ran through her mind as her urges grew. *Everyone has a drink now and then*, her habitual thoughts liked to assure her.

- In chapter 6, Lara's urges to spend hours on Facebook and reading celebrity gossip sites were accompanied by her inner lizard's mantra: *You won't be able to hold out all day. You might as well do it now and get it over with.* Her lizard liked to remind her how bad she was at dismissing her urges, making it sound like giving in was the only reasonable option.

- Jeremy's inner lizard (chapter 7) consistently and predictably sang a couple different songs that Jeremy could identify: *You're in trouble; the money is running out!* and *What's wrong with you for having these fears? You're really messed up.*

● For Valerie (chapter 9), who had a near-constant nagging that something dreadful might happen to her children, recognizing her inner lizard felt relatively easy. Any time she was imagining some scenario that was not currently happening, she knew it was only thought. If her children were safe, any thought that told her otherwise was her creative, active imagination at work and nothing to act on.

● In chapter 2, Nicole always felt rushed because her lower brain's favorite story was *Hurry! Go!* For her, what was most consistent and predictable was the feeling of urgency that accompanied her thinking. Once she noticed it, she became suspicious of anything said from that feeling. She began to use her urgency as a cue to slow down rather than speed up.

● Mario (chapter 11) experienced urges to gamble that promised, *This could turn it all around. This could be the big payday you've been waiting for.* As he recognized those empty promises, he found it far easier to dismiss them as his Addictive Voice than to confuse them with wisdom or his own common sense.

When you know what your lower brain says on repeat, you know what to dismiss. Consider making a note for yourself of your inner lizard's favorites.

Inner Lizard Thoughts Feel Different

In addition to their annoying consistency, there is another clear marker of inner lizard thoughts: when your mind is full of them, you probably don't feel your best.

You are always feeling your thinking. You feel nothing *but* your current thinking, actually. When your mind is flooded with habitual, conditioned, unhelpful lower-brain programming, you feel it. I can't tell you exactly what it will feel like, as it's different for each person, and it even changes slightly from moment to moment. It might feel like stress, urgency, anxiety, dread, or any number of things.

Because peace is your nature, and your set point is a calm, clear space, that's where you have the most access to your own common sense and wisdom. The thoughts and emotions you experience when you are quiet and tranquil are trustworthy. When you don't have that nice feeling, you are caught up in empty, habitual thought, and those stress-filled thoughts are not trustworthy.

Just as you can become familiar with the way your habit sounds and what it says, you can get to know the feeling of your habit as well. Notice how it feels mentally, emotionally, and physically. The tunes on your inner lizard's playlist may have a different tone and volume than the other thoughts you have, and they will almost certainly feel less peaceful.

Notice the tension, urgency, or fear your habit-related thoughts tend to produce and contrast that with how freedom from your habit feels. Take note of how it feels to be relaxed and comfortable, with a calm and clear mind. You can trust and respect your thoughts when you feel that way. And when you are feeling your habit-related thoughts, stop and wait for your mind to clear.

13

There Is Power in the Pause

Pausing before you act can change everything.

Let's look at two types of pause. The first is the pause taken consciously and purposely. When you feel an urge rising up, or you find yourself engaging in behaviors that tend to precede your habit, you decide to pause before you do anything more. You may not have perfect success each and every time, but perfection is irrelevant. *Intending* to pause will surely lead to more pausing than not even trying, and even imperfect, occasional pausing will keep you from acting on some urges.

The other kind of pause tends to occur more naturally and effortlessly, almost by default. When you see something deeper about the urges you experience, leading you to view them as habitual thought rather than meaningful or powerful messages, you pause automatically. This type of pause feels like it happens *for* you rather than *by* you. When you are deeply aware that urges aren't "you," acting on them isn't as compelling. You simply find yourself jumping into action far less. It would make no more sense to act on your every thought than it would to jump on every bus that passes your house. You will effortlessly find yourself letting those buses—the ones that take you toward your habit, or anywhere you don't want to go, for that matter—pass you by.

Of course, these are two ends of a spectrum, and your pause in any given moment may feel somewhere in the middle. Any type of pause is excellent. You might pause more deliberately at first and then find over time that it is becoming more natural and automatic. All that matters is that you wait and make sure you're getting on the bus that takes you where you want to go. Pause first, whatever that pause looks like, and you'll find yourself acting on urges far less.

The Choice Point

Marianne had been a compulsive collector for the better part of seventeen years. Initially, she had some interest in the things she was collecting—antique spoons, a particular type of collectible doll, vintage jewelry—but Marianne told me in our initial coaching session that the sense of collecting being a hobby faded after the first few years, and collecting began to feel more like a compulsion. Rather than being a source of joy, it turned into something she did in response to strong urges. She began doing her habit solely to make the urges go away.

It is worth noting that Marianne's habit of collecting things began after a particularly rough period in her life. The first antique spoons she acquired were family heirlooms that she received after the sudden death of both of her parents. For a while, collecting those spoons— and then other things—were associated with Marianne's past and her attempt to keep it alive in some way.

Throughout this book, I've stressed that habits are the result of thought—they are impersonal and temporary human experience. I've argued that we can come to see our habit and urges in a new way and that that insight itself can completely change things, with no particular requirement to first look for and resolve complex emotional issues. Once a habit is formed, it can be viewed as a series of habitual thoughts that feel uncomfortable and look dangerous or meaningful. It is also true that habits are our best attempt to feel good, like ourselves again. They often begin because we aren't comfortable in our skin in some way and because we have feelings or thoughts that we do not want to face. Habits are excellent distractions from inner experiences we don't like and, as I've said many times, they provide helpful information, a reminder that we should step back and allow our mind to naturally quiet.

So although I feel that the best way to initially treat a habit is as a series of impersonal thoughts that appear real, that doesn't mean that, as Marianne's coach, I would ignore the fact that her habit began for emotional reasons. Marianne and I talked about the thoughts that led her to begin collecting. We talked about her sense that continuing to collect was in some way keeping her past alive for her. In this particular case, those discussions were extremely helpful in giving Marianne a full picture of how her habit started. But just because her habit started as a way of helping her feel better when her feelings were low, that doesn't mean that any unhappiness she feels is a serious issue that only her habit can fix. Now that Marianne sees the truth about her innate peace of mind—that when she's feeling low, she's only feeling her thinking in that moment rather than a more stable life problem—she is better equipped to dismiss any urges that might arise when she is in a low mood.

She can grieve the loss of her parents in any way she needs to, and she can also recognize and dismiss her urges to collect things she doesn't want. Ultimately, she can step back when she senses the feelings associated with an urge rather than jump into action.

Our work together was always about helping Marianne see the source of her suffering and the truth about her innate health and resilience. When she saw that her suffering came from old thoughts about her parents and from taking her urges as meaningful "truth" that had to be obeyed, those thoughts and urges felt less gripping. As they loosened their grasp on her, Marianne suddenly had some choice in which thoughts she wanted to act on and which she wanted to dismiss.

After we spent some time working together, and once Marianne had learned the ideas I've been sharing in this book, Marianne's urges to add to her collections felt less consuming and overwhelming. She rarely felt hijacked by urges the way she once had, but the urges hadn't completely gone away. She still experienced occasional strong urges and frequent weaker ones, though she was learning to see the truth about them more clearly and to act on them less.

As she grew increasingly aware of her urges and less intimidated by them, Marianne noticed a "choice point."

She saw that there was a moment when she was experiencing an urge—but had not yet acted on it—when a window seemed to open up. This was a relatively small window of time in which she had the ability to make a choice: to obey or not to obey.

The truth is that any moment can be a choice point. No matter where you are in the life cycle of an urge or how far you've stepped into actually acting out your habit, you can have a moment of clarity. It's not uncommon to recognize one or more choice points in hindsight. Looking back, you might remember a one- or two-second pause before you launched into your habit. You might recall asking yourself if you were actually going to go through with it. Personally, I can remember many times when I was driving to buy food when my wisdom would speak up, saying, *Just go home. You don't have to go through with this.* But because I didn't yet realize that the urge would fade on its own if I turned around and went home, those voices felt taunting. It was a pipe dream to think I could actually change course mid-urge. Now, however, I see that it only felt that way because of how I was relating to the urge. Because I believed that the urge was meaningful, powerful, and would only go away if I binged, I shot my own wisdom down as soon as it came up.

Any thought that suggests that you don't need to obey your urge is inner wisdom. I find it incredible that in the middle of a strong urge, with all of that confusing, swirling thought spinning around, wisdom still peeks through. That speaks to your resilience. You are fueled by wisdom. It is what you are—your true nature—underneath your moment-to-moment thinking. Any little break in that rush of thought is an opportunity for wisdom to shine through.

Sometimes you follow wisdom, and sometimes you turn away from it. All that truly matters is that you see that wisdom is there for you. The more you learn to rely on it, the more you will naturally find yourself guided by it.

It is often easier to notice your choice point and take a pause when there is some space between "you" and your urges. That space comes from having seen a new truth about urges and sometimes also from having begun to dismiss them. When Marianne stopped acting on all of her urges, she gained that space—an awareness of herself and her situation—and that allowed her to become increasingly aware of her choice point, between when her urge began and when she acted on it. She could pause, listen to wisdom, and make a choice in that moment if she chose to. Luckily, for Marianne, she did choose to pause, and her habit quickly began to retreat.

Veto Power

The concept of "free won't," also referred to as "veto power" (Kühn and Brass 2009), was briefly touched on in chapter 10. Free won't is your free will *not* to act on urges or thoughts. Universal mind, operating through your prefrontal cortex (part of what we've been calling the *higher brain,* which is in charge of decision making and coordinated action), gives you the power of choice. Even when you can't see the choices you have, you do have the ability to choose to do nothing about an urge or thought you feel. The more you exercise free won't and make the choice to pause and not obey your urges, the weaker your urges become. In spiritual terms, letting those thoughts come and go without viewing them as meaningful or reflective of "you" allows you to more clearly notice the innate wisdom that lies beneath them. When your mind is not clutching at the thoughts rushing through it, it rests in something deeper, truer, and far more helpful.

Cultivating that pause leads to longer and longer pauses and increasing feelings of choice. At first,

Marianne would call me and say, "I gave in to the urge; I bought another spoon today." I would ask if she had noticed a choice point, a moment when she *chose* to give in to her urge. Sometimes she had and other times she had not.

As she continued pausing to dismiss the urge when she could, she noticed her choice point much more often. Even better, she increasingly made the choice in that moment not to obey the urge. At times, the process was a little confusing for Marianne. She initially believed that if she were truly seeing her urge as meaningless, fleeting "neurological junk," her urges wouldn't cause her tension or be persuasive at all. But that's not always the case. Your brain is used to your habit. It has been producing urges that have been obeyed for some time. Although your brain can definitely change, it loves efficiency and won't necessarily *want* to change. But remember, change is always possible through the universal, spiritual energy that powers your physical brain.

Marianne came to see that not giving in to urges can be relatively effortless, but isn't always so. At times, not giving in to an urge takes some effort—you may need to look for and practice a more deliberate pause to some extent until you settle into a new normal.

With some time, though, Marianne got to the point that as soon as her urges began, her mind turned to the pause. She would notice an urge, instantly remember that it was a fleeting, self-correcting human experience, and see if she could reach for that choice point. When she sensed her power to make a choice, she made the choice to not obey the urge. That choice—and the release of tension that came as her urge began to fade—was exhilarating for Marianne. It was for me too. I remember dismissing my urges to binge and feeling so excited and proud of myself, knowing that my choices were physically changing the landscape of my brain.

It is sometimes easy, sometimes difficult, and everything in between. In time, Marianne stopped obeying all of her urges, and her urges stopped showing up. Recognizing the power in the pause was an enormous help in that process.

14

There Is Nothing You Must Do

Throughout this book, I've talked about insight as the primary tool in changing your habit. When you truly see that you are fundamentally well by nature, and you come to see your habit as made of temporary thought that covers your innate wellness, your habit begins to look and feel very different. It becomes less persuasive, less stable, and something that is far easier to dismiss. And when you dismiss the thought that drives your habit enough, your habit tends to fall away.

Insight is an oddly passive process. As discussed in chapter 5, there are things we can do to open ourselves to insight. Just by reading this book, you are doing that. But by and large, the approach I've shared with you is relatively passive. It is far more passive than other approaches.

I understand it can be baffling to hear that there is nothing you must do to end your habit. When you're used to taking charge and making things happen, it makes sense that your habit would look like something that requires fixing and that you are the one who should do that fixing—with the emphasis on *doing* something. "Seeing things in a new way" and "waiting for an insight" can feel ineffective at best, and like resignation or powerlessness at worst.

When I talk about dismissing a painful thought or an urge to do something you don't want to do, sometimes people hear that as *ignoring* a thought or an urge. But actually, dismissing and ignoring are polar opposites. The difference is rooted in what you believe about people and problems.

If you believe that the fundamental nature of all humans is clarity and wellness and that that nature never changes, though it can be temporarily covered with whatever happens to be on our minds in any given moment, habits—by definition—are thought. *Temporary* thought, to boot.

Sometimes you feel gripped by your habit and sometimes you don't, right? Our experience, including our habits (which are just more ebbing and flowing experience), is far more in flux than it looks, far more fluid than we've been told. When you're given a diagnosis like I was—or you come to think of yourself as a "gambler" like Mario did, a "hoarder" like Marianne, a "worrier" like Valerie and Jeremy, or an "insecure codependent who needs constant reassurance from a partner" like Jackie—you lose sight of the fact that your habit comes and goes. It begins to feel like the habit is a stable part of you, always there, albeit sometimes in the background.

In truth, your habit will change as your thinking changes. What is there to fix when you are well at your core, but just underneath a passing cloud of thought? You don't need to help the clouds pass. You have no part in their passing. Habits are a function of the mind, so when your mind quiets down, your habit is transformed. I hope "there is nothing you must do" is beginning to make more sense.

When I was struggling with my binge-eating habit, I argued that the "thought clouds" that made binge eating feel so unavoidable *didn't* pass, move, or change. It felt like they hovered over me for years, barely moving. Even when the clouds did break up here and there—enough that I could clearly see the blue sky and bright sun behind them—they would always roll back in, as I knew they would.

Now, I can see my role in that experience. Because I didn't view my habit as thought and didn't fully grasp the extent of my innate mental health and capacity for resilience, my habit looked far more meaningful and stable than it truly was. I had a diagnosis, after all. It looked like a "disorder," with known symptoms and a predictable trajectory and prognosis, and my expectations for how it was supposed to look loomed large in my mind. The clouds did part occasionally, and I did enjoy moments—even days or weeks—of freedom from the revved-up mind that resulted in binge eating. But I never saw myself as free. I was always looking over my shoulder, waiting for urges to strike, believing that when they did, I'd have no choice but to give in. My expectations were so strong that I innocently brought back those clouds. I viewed myself as so stuck that I *couldn't* have experienced anything else.

When you believe that you are capable of being stuck or damaged or that all problems require tangible, real-world, action-oriented solutions, "doing nothing" looks like neglect or laziness. That's why we so quickly jump into action, looking for the "three-step solution" or "ten-day fix" to our "problem."

But if those three-step solutions and ten-day fixes worked—even if they only worked for *most people*—we'd all be doing them with great success.

Behavior change is the consequence, not the solution. Behavior changes as a result of seeing things differently. When it works in that direction, change is deep and lasting.

What You Can Do Versus What You Must Do

It's never that you can't or shouldn't do anything. If something occurs to you that looks helpful, by all means, do it. That inclination to act may be your wisdom. Please, follow your own hunches. *Doing something* might look like taking a pause before you act on your habit, or noticing your inner lizard's favorite tunes; or it might look like going for a walk, calling a friend, or taking a nap. It could look like anything, really.

The point is this: You *can* do anything that feels right in the moment, but there is nothing you *must* do. You have no job here. Your innate health is covered. Do what you're inclined to do to help yourself, but there is no one thing that everyone *must* do.

You are a part of nature, and nature has a self-correcting mechanism built in. Nature has a bent toward thriving, and you do too. So when I suggest that you dismiss your urge to beat yourself up or that you dismiss your urge to quiet your mind with a box of doughnuts or a bottle of wine or that you dismiss your urge to run away from your marriage, job, or responsibilities, I'm certainly not saying to ignore your urges for those things. To *dismiss* them is to see that they are created by thought and that, as your mind self-corrects, those things will naturally look different. To *ignore* them is to truly believe something needs attention and to fail to give it attention.

Dismissing is to see the truth that we come equipped with a self-correcting mechanism and that not everything needs a human fix. Ignoring uses effort and energy. Dismissing is effortless. It frees you up and takes the job of managing your experience off your plate.

The more you remember that you really are well and healthy underneath the surface chaos, the more natural and obvious doing nothing will be.

Thought and urges fade. Let the inner lizard lose its voice, and *then* listen to what occurs to you. There is nothing more you must do.

15

Understanding Thought Changes Everything

Joan was convinced that none of her neighbors liked her. She was flooded with fears about being left out or disliked. When Joan noticed a couple of the neighborhood women chatting at the end of their driveways, her mind spun stories of them becoming quick, close friends who would never let her into their circle. When Joan's neighbors invited her over for coffee, she assumed that they simply felt bad for her or were too polite to exclude her altogether. Anything her neighbors did—even when it was inclusive—Joan saw as an example of their disapproval. She entertained those interpretations and bought into them, for the most part.

You see, Joan also knew better. Joan and I had been working together for nearly a year, and in that time, she had come to see that the stories that spun through her mind were not reflective of reality.

Joan had had this particular thought-habit since she was eight years old—thirty-five years ago—when she was rejected by some girls at school. Joan clearly remembered the details of that day when the girl who had been her best friend became friends with some girls in the "cool" group, leaving her behind. That's where habitual thoughts like *I don't measure up* and *Why would they like me?* began.

Joan is beginning to glimpse a deeper truth about the nature of habitual thought. The truth that is beginning to come into focus will help her to naturally let some of those thoughts go. That truth can eventually set Joan free.

Presence Is Not the Problem

As you've seen thus far in this book, the mere presence of thought is not a problem. Thoughts and urges are part of being human. It's only what you *make of* those thoughts or urges—what you believe about them and how you relate to and interact with them—that matters.

Thought is vaporous, like a cloud. From a distance, clouds look solid and substantial. But as you get closer—as the airplane you're on flies through the middle of one—you realize there is nothing solid or stable about it.

The same is true of thoughts and urges. They are vaporous, far less solid and significant than they appear. The problem is that when thought *appears* solid, you treat it as if it is. You mistakenly believe you can protect yourself from painful thoughts by resisting or denying them or by replacing them with happier thoughts. You try to push thoughts away, move them along, or even remind yourself incessantly that they are "only thought" or that "it's all temporary," when they feel anything but. This seems helpful on the face of it, but it is another way we innocently imbue vaporous thought with attention (remember, *insightfully seeing* thought as temporary and safe is very different than actively reminding yourself or trying to convince yourself of that truth).

When you take those well-meaning actions, you shower your thoughts and urges with attention, which ends up giving you the opposite of what you want. You focus on your thoughts when you judge or try to fix them, turning vapor into what feels like concrete. Your attempts to manage your mind and your emotions backfire, and the very thoughts you are trying to shrink are magnified in your consciousness.

The attention and focus you place on your thoughts is what gives you the sticky experience you have of them. Pretty ironic, isn't it? The very thing you're trying to avoid, you're unknowingly creating. When you see the nature of thought enough to remove your focus, those thoughts feel fluid again.

Joan knew the truth about her thoughts in a conceptual sense, but she didn't have much firsthand experience of them ebbing and flowing on their own. She was afraid of her painful thoughts because her experience was one of being deeply affected by them. She often felt stuck in them, and that perceived stuckness meant hours—sometimes days—of feeling horrible about herself.

Because Joan dreaded the *presence* of her insecure thoughts, she shut down when they arose. She denied how she was feeling. She frantically did other things in an attempt to distract herself from what was on her mind, rather than seeing her feelings as an invitation to step back and let her mind naturally calm down. And although those actions were an attempt at feeling better, they were actually making for a harder experience for

Joan. Each time Joan reacted to her urges so strongly, she suffered more.

Joan is certainly not alone. Lara (chapter 6) spent hours online reading celebrity and Facebook gossip. Lara's urges themselves weren't the real problem—she intuitively knew that it was the hopeless, victim-like way she related to them that gave them all of their power. The moment she noticed a thought like *You can just log on for a minute*, she would find herself in a panic, her mind racing, wondering why this was happening to her, and accepting the fact that she had wasted another day surfing the Net before she had even acted on the urge. That way of treating a fleeting urge, as if it is a real, stable, done deal, is what ultimately keeps us locked in habits.

Jeremy (chapter 7) was plagued by habitual thoughts about losing all of his money. The way he explains it, the fear of losing his money was only half of his "problem"; the more painful part was that he thought he was going crazy for having these recurring thoughts in the first place. Jeremy's wisdom told him that he was doing the best he could financially and that his best was better than most. But he also took his fears seriously in some ways, assuming that the presence of those habitual thoughts meant that they were a "sign" of something he should pay attention to or that he was on the verge of going crazy.

Jeremy did a lot of thinking *about* his thinking. He made so much of his mental state that he unknowingly made things worse for himself, treating his financial fears as cement—because that's how they felt—rather than like the vaporous, temporary thoughts they truly were.

All we have to do is see the truth about thought. When we see a deeper truth about the impersonal, ebbing-and-flowing nature of our human experience, we find it much easier to let those thoughts stay vaporous. We have no problem when urges come and go—presence is not the problem.

Attention, focus, and viewing thoughts as stable and substantial are the only "problems," and those are easily remedied with the understanding you are gaining.

PART III

LIFELONG

CHANGE

16

It Gets Easier

As time goes on, leaving your habit behind becomes far easier than it is at the outset. This may sound obvious, but it is a fact that is easy to overlook.

The way it may be now—actively taking those pauses before you act; dismissing urges in perhaps a more purposeful, hit-or-miss way; your mind still naturally gravitating toward habitual thoughts about your habit that feel real and action-worthy—is not how it will be forever.

When you forget that, it is all too easy to give up. It's easy to think, *This is too hard. I don't want to feel like this forever.* But it won't feel like this forever. Your habit provides a quick fix for terrible discomforts that can often feel too much to bear. But you can experience a new normal, one in which your mind slows down and you feel more comfortable within yourself. There will be a day when your habit is no longer on your mind.

There will be a shift at some point, and you'll feel like your habit is behind you. That won't mean you are immune from ever stumbling back into your habit; it just means that things will feel different. The shift will feel substantial, as if your foundation has changed. You will come to see your urges, your habit, and your capacity for resilience in a different way. If you are *really* blessed, you will see life in a different way. You will begin to rest easier, knowing that you are going to be okay, no matter what happens in the future.

The spiritual principles in this book are giving you a peek behind the curtain at the *system* that explains what it means to be human. Understanding the underlying system allows for foundational shifts that reach far beyond specific behaviors.

I remember the day I learned a few basic principles about baking—why baked goods rise and why they fail to rise, how baking powder is different from baking soda, and so on. Before that, most of what I baked turned out the way I wanted it to, but every once in a while, it didn't. When it didn't, I was baffled. Because I didn't know what the problem was, I felt like the victim of invisible baking saboteurs who snuck into the oven and ruined my creations.

Once I learned a few simple principles about baking, I no longer felt like a victim in the same way. I had a deeper understanding of how the underlying system worked, and that understanding helped immensely. It didn't mean I never made baking mistakes again, but when I did, I could typically see where I went wrong, and I no longer felt helpless or powerless about it. There was a system to understand; there was *something reliable to see*.

The same thing happened when I saw that my urges to binge were neurological junk that would fade on their own. I became excited about experiencing them and letting them fade, because I knew that would eventually mean the end of my habit. In many ways, things were never the same again. I still experienced urges for a while, and they were still uncomfortable. Because our moment-to-moment thinking is what we feel, I felt my fair share of that moment-to-moment thinking. But the foundation had shifted such that I knew there were *principles at play*—similar to those principles of baking I had learned—that were dependable and unwavering. I had had a peek into the system, and understanding the system took away the panic and powerlessness. Even when my temporary thoughts looked real, and even when I got caught up in them and binged, I knew that the foundation had shifted and that things were changing.

That shift will happen for you as well, and when it does, things will get easier. How you relate to your habit is always evolving. Some people experience it as a series of steps, each one helping you reach new levels of freedom from your habit. Others experience it as one big leap. Some go only forward; others go forward, sometimes slip back, and then move forward again. Your path will be unique to you, but know that you are on a path. If you keep looking in this direction, at these principles and truths about yourself and your habit, you will continue seeing more, and what you see will help you.

A New Normal

I started smoking cigarettes in college. In graduate school, I knew it was time to quit.

I didn't have the understanding shared in this book, unfortunately. I *knew* (or thought that I knew) that quitting would be a hard feat that required discipline and willpower. Everything I had read and heard told me that it would be a long, painful struggle to white-knuckle my way through cravings until they stopped coming around. I had tried to quit twice before, but this time I was up for the challenge, ready to suffer for the greater good of my long-term health.

By far, the biggest obstacle—the one I couldn't quite make it past in my previous attempts to quit—was that I loved the feeling I got from smoking. I didn't like smoking itself, but I loved the relaxed, peaceful feeling it gave me. Cigarettes were an escape. After a tough class, a big presentation, or a few hours holed away in the psychology lab, lighting up was my mind's cue to let it all go. I left my thinking behind and relaxed in a way that I desperately needed.

I didn't crave the nicotine as much as I craved the release of tension. Although I knew the benefits of quitting would outweigh the cost, the cost seemed gigantic. The "cost," as I saw it, was my ability to let go and relax. I imagined that as a nonsmoker, I'd be uptight and tense, though with very clean lungs.

I have heard countless people express the same concern about leaving their habit behind. "Where will my peace and relaxation come from?" they ask. "How will I escape my busy, chatty mind? What about the wonderful feeling I get from my habit? Will I ever feel that way again?"

Remember, it gets easier. Things change, shifts occur, a new normal is reached (and then surpassed), and you won't need your habit to relax and feel good. You're used to tying your feelings of relaxation to your habit, but the truth is that all good feelings come from within you. When your mind quiets down, you feel good. You've been using your habit to quiet your mind, but in the absence of your habit, you will have the opportunity to let your mind quiet itself naturally, the way it is designed to—especially now that you understand that your mind has a self-correcting mechanism built in. That clarity can become your new normal.

As I prepared to break my smoking habit for the third time, I read a book called *Allen Carr's Easy Way to Stop Smoking* (2004). Carr's method looks at why people continue to smoke rather than why they should quit. Not surprisingly, one of the top reasons smokers continue to smoke was my concern exactly—cigarettes are their pathway to peace and relaxation.

Carr's essential message is that once the nicotine habit is broken, a new normal is reached, and former smokers actually do enjoy peace and relaxation; but now it comes from within themselves, without the need for cigarettes. In the terms we've been using in this book, it is important to know that *a large portion of the relaxation and pleasant feelings that come from your habit—no matter what your habit is—is the release of the tension created by the urge.* That means that once the urges are gone, there will be less tension to release. You will still experience stress and tension in your life, of course, but those feelings will come and go—as they do for everyone. You will begin to bounce back to your default state more naturally, without relying on your habit.

When your new normal is urge-free, your habit will have no reason to exist. When your lower brain is no longer holding on to that habit, you will arrive at a peaceful feeling and a quiet mind in different, healthier ways. You will be able to use the presence of discomfort to see that you are innocently using your power of thought against yourself, and you'll be able to step back and let your mind refresh on its own.

The foundation shifts, and your relaxation comes from within you rather than from obeying an urge. Although it looks like your habit creates positive feelings, it actually creates uncomfortable feelings (urges) and then shows you how to relieve that pain. You aren't relaxing as much as you are coming back up to baseline.

As you leave your habit behind, your baseline shifts upward, and you begin to feel better more and more.

You will reach a new level, a new normal, where you get to encounter the full range of human experience without being tied to a habit. And that new normal is well worth the levels you leaped to get there.

17

Setbacks Are Meaningless

Let's imagine that you've read the first sixteen chapters in this book and that your habit has died down. You've seen urges in a new way—as a fleeting thought that operates like an alarm clock, and as a powerless inner lizard that will lose its voice if you don't apply the sticky agent of attention and resistance—and so you're not bound to act on urges the way you once were.

As you occasionally dismiss those urges, they change. You're no longer turning them into what feels like cement; you're letting them remain vaporous, and as such, they tend to break up and go away. You are increasingly habit-free, and life is feeling easier than it has in years.

Then one day, out of nowhere, you fall into your habit again. In a moment of temporary confusion, you obsess about your children's safety, your financial future, how your neighbors feel about you, or how you spend money or waste hours online.

When I work with clients who are leaving old habits behind, this happens *all the time*. It's the rule more often than the exception, so I have absolutely no concerns when a client comes to me after months of being habit-free and says, "I did it again."

Take a second and let that sink in, because it may be one of the most important things you read in this book. Falling back into habitual behavior is the rule, not the exception, and it means absolutely nothing. It is a reflection of the fact that your mind got very full and busy—nothing else.

Although I have no concerns, my clients, on the other hand, are typically mortified. They want to know what happened and why their change didn't stick. They become convinced that recovery is not possible for them and that this setback predicts their future. They say things like "I knew this was too good to be true" or "There's no way kicking a habit is that simple."

Their reactions are perfectly understandable, but misinformed. Societal norms and some popular addiction treatments have set up a black-and-white, do-or-die sort of mentality when it comes to habits. We're on the wagon or we're off; we're in the clear or we're in the weeds. But that's only one way of thinking about it, and it is not always accurate or helpful.

What is much more accurate—and infinitely more helpful—is the understanding that falling back into your habit at some point is not only really, really common, but also totally and completely meaningless.

The Lower Brain

Think back to what you know about the lower brain. It is machinelike and highly suggestible. It latches on to thoughts and behaviors—especially those that pack an emotional and neurochemical punch—and spins them into patterns and conditioned responses. Of course, you are never locked in any feeling or thought solely because of your brain's actions. The brain is a physical machine that was created and is powered by something *far* more powerful. That spiritual energy, or universal mind, makes any experience possible, regardless of what the brain does. But in very limited brain science terms, your brain has a propensity to repeat patterns and create habits.

The more consistent a thought or behavior is, the stronger the neural pathways representing that thought or behavior tend to be. Imagine walking through the woods. If you walk through the woods along exactly the same route every day, your footsteps will start to beat a path through the grass and weeds. Over time, as that path becomes more pronounced, it becomes the obvious go-to trail, the path of least resistance. Your chances of taking another path through the woods—one still tangled with weeds—decrease, and your natural proclivity toward the beaten path grows.

In a sense, a similar thing happens in your brain when you've been thinking the same things over and over (*especially* when you've been fueling them with attention, turning them into neural superglue) or engaging in the same behaviors repeatedly. You "wear down" neural pathways in your brain, making your habitual thoughts and behaviors the easiest, most natural and accessible choice. Even after you've managed to largely move past your habit, there may still be a path of least resistance in your brain, which can make it easy to find yourself in your habit again if you don't have a deeper understanding of what is possible *beyond* the brain.

I've worked with clients who have been struggling with the same habit for forty years. That's forty years of walking the same path through the woods. But whether it's been forty years or forty days, the grass won't grow over your beaten path overnight. It only makes sense that you might find yourself falling into those well-practiced thoughts and behaviors again at some point.

Even after a profound insight—and even after a long period of time dismissing urges, not having urges, or not engaging in your habit—it isn't particularly shocking that the urge might randomly strike and that you might find yourself acting on it.

Luckily, it is perfectly okay if you do.

The Stories We Tell About Setbacks

Annie's habit involved her hands. Without even realizing she was doing it, she would bite her fingernails and the area around them until they bled. She would also crack her knuckles and wring her hands, applying enormous pressure to them until they were swollen and sore.

Annie wondered whether her habit was even treatable, since much of her behavior was done without her conscious consent. Biting, cracking, and wringing her hands was what she "found herself" doing, and she often didn't wake up to the fact that she was doing it until she had been at it for some time.

Nevertheless, the more we talked about the nature of her habit, and the more aware Annie became of the feelings that accompanied her habitual behaviors, the faster she began catching herself in the throes of it. I encouraged Annie to do her best to stop as soon as she noticed the urge or the behavior, knowing that her innate health would do its part and that she would eventually begin catching herself hurting her hands sooner and sooner. That's exactly what happened. Within a few months, Annie's nail biting had been drastically reduced, and the knuckle cracking and hand wringing had nearly stopped altogether. She was thrilled.

Then, a few months later, she sent me a panicked e-mail. She was at it again, she said. "Back at square one," she wrote, "as if all our work together has been for nothing."

Here's what actually happened. One day, as Annie—who is a lawyer—was working on a very important legal brief, she starting biting her nails. As was common for her, she didn't notice right away. It wasn't until a drop of blood from her bleeding cuticles dropped onto her laptop keyboard that she realized what she had been doing.

Maybe it was because Annie was already in a low state of mind, stressed about the brief she was working on, or maybe it was the sight of blood that set her off, or

183

the fact that she had just been celebrating how nonexistent her habit had become—whatever it was, Annie reacted to her "setback" in a big way. She was convinced that her progress was all for nothing, that she'd never stop her habitual behaviors, and that she was a fool for being so proud of herself. That's how it looked to her in that moment.

In the days that followed, Annie became aware of herself beginning to bite her nails again. But rather than noticing the urge and dismissing it, she gave in to it. *What's the use?* she thought. From her defeated state of mind, everything looked like a sign of how far gone she was.

It's easy to see how the way Annie interpreted that single setback took her off track. It wasn't her behavior that hurt her, but the meaning she gave that behavior. But it didn't have to be that way.

Viewing Setbacks as Normal and Meaningless

When Annie and I had an "emergency session," as she called it, I said something like this to her:

"What if, when you were working on your brief and saw that drop of blood hit your keyboard, you happened to have a different thought?

"There is absolutely nothing wrong with the thoughts you had. This isn't about blame or even changing or correcting yourself as much as it is about seeing how the meaning you attached to that innocent little drop of blood changed the trajectory of the next few weeks for you.

"Seeing that one instance of biting your nails as important and meaningful *made* it important and meaningful. If you had thought, *Oops, I guess I was biting my nails again!* and simply stopped, the following days would have been different. If you had found compassion for yourself and thought, *Wow, I must be feeling a lot of stress!*—or patience with yourself and thought, *I'm biting my nails now, but I know exactly what to do from here!*—everything may have been different. You might have stopped as soon as you noticed yourself hurting your hands and been able to dismiss any later urges you had. My hunch is that had you done that, you would have very quickly found yourself where you were before the blood hit the keyboard: habit-free.

"There truly is no problem. Most people fall back into habitual thoughts and behaviors at times. We are human beings, not perfectly consistent or predictable robots. You innocently taught yourself to hurt your hands simply by doing it repeatedly, and you are in the process of teaching your brain to *not* do it. It is a *process*. You're doing excellently—as well as you were doing before this setback."

Annie heard something in what I said.

She saw how her response to falling back into her habit was the sole problem. Her inconsistency was not a problem at all. Her behaviors didn't indicate anything significant about her or her future. She had simply bitten her nails again, end of story.

So Annie began again—she dismissed her urges the best she could, and in very little time, she was right back to where she had been: habit-free.

18

Forget What You Think You Know

One of my mentors calls it "showing up dumb."

You do it when you leave your personal, opinionated, judgmental thinking behind—as much as one can, anyway—and show up open in the moment. When you show up "dumb," without a lot of personal ideas cluttering your mind, you get to discover life as it truly is. When you show up "smart," full of your own beliefs and ideas, you don't discover anything. Instead, you tend to just confirm what your own mind already thinks it knows.

Discovering is very different from confirming. Discovering leads to change; confirming leads to more of the same. Given that you're here for change, discovering is definitely the way to go. Wisdom, common sense, and helpful ideas are available to you at all times. When your mind is relatively free of personal thought, you're bound to discover them.

When you listen to what experts say about breaking your habit—even though their insights don't resonate with you—you're ignoring your own inner guidance in favor of someone's personal thinking. Showing up dumb—unattached to others' opinions—allows you to find the path that works for you.

When your habit makes you sick or feels awful in some other way but you continue to do it, it is your habitual thinking that is leading the charge, drowning out your own common sense. What gets in the way of health, peace, and clarity is personal thinking—that stuff that makes us "smart." As you begin to hold what you think you know more loosely, considering that maybe things aren't always as they seem, you make room for new thought. You are guided by something far wiser than intellect.

The less you think you know, the freer you are, and the more you discover.

• • •

I came to see this "the less you think you know, the freer you are" truth very clearly with my own binge-eating habit.

For years, I thought I knew exactly what my body needed to look and function the way I *thought* was best. I believed I needed to nearly always eat healthy food (and, of course, I made up the definition for what was "healthy food"). Only very occasional less healthy treats were allowed. I thought I should never eat when I wasn't hungry unless it was a rare and special occasion. My personal thinking also told me that I needed to exercise for an hour a day, at least six days a week, and that the exercise needed to be hard, not fun.

Looking back, it's amazing how specific and regimented my "recipe for success" was in my mind. It looked to me that if I followed those made-up rules to the letter, I would maintain my weight. If I veered off of that plan even just a little, I wouldn't.

You may be looking at my rules, thinking *Of course you believed that. Those* are *things that lead to being healthy and fit.* They certainly are not counterintuitive. There are many experts who would say that those things are helpful, maybe even necessary ingredients for maintaining your weight and being in shape. The thing is, there is scientific evidence for nearly *every* opinion out there, especially with regard to physical health, weight, and fitness. You will find experts who agree with pretty much any thought you have. What one expert swears by (carbs, intense cardiovascular exercise, or caffeine), another expert rejects.

My problem was that I only looked at one side of that equation. I could find experts who agreed with each of my personal opinions, and I found scientific evidence that corroborated everything I thought, so I stopped there. In some cases, I didn't even realize there were opposing viewpoints. I made the advice of *some* experts confirm that what I was doing was right, and I completely missed the fact that it was only personal thought I was clutching to. In hindsight, I can see how my wisdom actually did try to speak up. I did have the occasional sense that there had to be an easier way, but I let my personal thinking override it.

I can now see that I was clutching to my own personal thought. The fact that my diet and fitness regime felt so bad is an indication that I was relying on my own thoughts instead of wisdom and truth. I was certain it was necessary, but my relationship with food and exercise felt harsh and restrictive. It required enormous amounts of discipline and energy. It was not natural by a long shot. My wisdom and common sense told me—often, actually—that this was no way to live. But I dismissed that wisdom, because I was afraid to loosen my grip on what I *thought* was the best way forward.

It can be difficult to tease apart personal thought that seems indisputable with truth or wisdom, but luckily, you don't need to do that. You only have to be willing to be wrong about what you think you know and let something clearer and more certain rise to the surface. The *feeling*, especially feelings of peace and clarity, will show you the difference. When you are willing to look beyond your own subjective logic and intellect to something that speaks to you in a deeper way, you will hear it.

When I stopped believing my own made-up rules about what my body needed, and I admitted that I didn't know anything for sure, my body showed me what it wanted and needed. Not all at once, but over time, a series of insights and questions occurred to me that led me to a very different place.

As it turns out, I actually could enjoy dessert regularly and have fun, moderate workouts and still—quite easily—maintain my natural weight. As soon as I loosened the grip I had on my old way of thinking, these possibilities arose. When I asked myself, *What if I'm wrong about these things that feel so difficult?* I stopped confirming and was free to discover. The wisdom within me pointed me toward choices that felt right for me. My common sense led the way. I began eating and moving in ways that occurred to me to eat and move, and it felt easier and freer, like I was getting closer to *home*.

It was not always easy to dismiss the personal thinking that told me that *it* knew better. I certainly don't want to suggest that this was easy, but I did feel myself moving toward something that felt more natural.

There Is No Past

One of the many things we become "smart" about—and therefore clutter our minds with—is thoughts of the past. We carry the past with us, applying it to our clean, blank-slate future.

Think of how you often wake up in the morning with a nice feeling, without a lot on your mind. As the seconds pass, while you're still lying in your warm, cozy bed, thoughts of yesterday's shopping binge, drinking, anger, or insecurity float into your mind. Those are memories—fleeting, passing thoughts that you experience in the moment but are about things that are no longer your current reality. Their only reality is as thought.

You innocently keep dragging those thoughts around, dredging them back up just as they begin to pass. When you feel free from the thoughts, you call that "being out of touch" or "ignoring the issue," and you drag those thoughts back into your mind. I almost felt as if it was my responsibility to feel bad the morning after a binge, as if that shameful feeling would somehow protect me in the future. Many of my clients report a similar thing. But wallowing in painful thoughts about something that is not currently happening serves no useful purpose. It can only hurt you.

If you mistakenly see that flood of painful thoughts about the past as reality, you have it all wrong. Those times when your "smart" personal thinking quiets down and you feel relative peace and calm are reality. The way you habitually carry memories of your habit around with you is how you *mask* reality and live in your head.

You aren't in charge of every thought that arises within you. But insightfully seeing how you innocently grab on to those thoughts and carry them around will quite naturally help you to do it far less. Seeing the truth about how thought operates makes space for you to hold your thinking more loosely, to be "dumber" in the moment.

And showing up dumb, with memories of the past seen for what they are and a clean slate in front of you, is exactly what you need to leave everything related to your habit behind you for good.

19

Build Healthy, Inside-Out Habits

Most of the goals we set and the positive habits we try to form are done with the expectation of a better life in the end.

It often looks as if happiness and satisfaction come from outside us. When we optimize our circumstances, we feel happy. When our circumstances are lacking, we suffer. If we could get the outside just right, we reason, the inner experiences of joy and contentment we dream about would be ours at last.

If you partner with the right person, choose the right career, live in the right place, and have the right family, friends, or hobbies, you can expect to experience more lasting satisfaction with life. And on the flip side, you can easily find lists of life stressors, circumstances that "create" stress. Too many of those, you're told, and you're bound to suffer.

The belief that our outer conditions are responsible for how we feel is unbelievably pervasive, but it is a misunderstanding. Our experience of life is not created from the outside in. How we feel cannot possibly come from the things around us. Rather, we experience life from the inside out. We feel our own moment-to-moment thinking, and those thoughts and feelings create our experiences. It only works in that direction.

When you consider the outside-in misunderstanding we innocently fall prey to, it's no wonder our goals and healthy habits fail to deliver the fulfillment we expect them to. Here's how it usually goes: you set out to form a healthy habit—let's say it's to drink more water: eight glasses a day, or whatever current opinion tells you is best.

It's a noble goal and has many of the traditional (mythical) markers of lasting happiness—you'll be healthier and happier, have more energy and glowing skin, and maybe drop a couple pounds, and everyone will love you. Not really, but that's how it feels with an outside-in goal.

You chose the goal because of the feelings you thought it would provide. But your moment-to-moment happiness in life comes from what's on your mind, not the glow of your skin or the admiration of your friends. Both hydrated and dehydrated people have thinking that goes up and down; we all experience only what's on our mind in each and every moment.

That's not to say that drinking more water wouldn't feel great. You would most likely feel better physically and be proud of yourself for forming the healthy habit. It's just that those feelings won't last forever. And when the change and initial excitement wear off and your thoughts return to their habitual set point, you find yourself feeling the same as you always did, albeit with more fluids in your system.

If your goal or habit was something you accomplished because you expected to feel better forever, you may be in for a rude awakening when the excitement wears off. If you are trapped within the outside-in misunderstanding, you will expect that accomplishing a goal will dramatically improve your life, and when it doesn't, it sets off a new set of alarm bells. Confused thinking takes over: *What's the problem? Did I choose the wrong goal? Since this goal or habit isn't providing the feeling I expected it to, maybe I got the goal wrong.*

At this point, many people set a new goal—one they are more confident will deliver a sustainably happy and successful feeling—and set out to accomplish that one. *I guess more water wasn't quite it. What I really wanted was to start doing yoga.* (Or complete a triathlon, travel the world, start meditating, write a book, get married, have an affair, get divorced, or any one of a number of ideas they had mentally attached with a particular feeling.) This is how we fall into the trap of chasing things outside of ourselves and feeling continually dissatisfied with how we feel. We wonder why we can't get it right, but we fail to recognize that we're shaking the wrong tree.

Living

I hope it doesn't sound like I'm down on setting goals, building healthy habits, or striving for things. Doing, accomplishing, and getting stuff out in the world is fun; doing and creating are part of the joy of being alive. But this is only when we don't use them as a means for something they will not provide.

If goals, habits, and external conditions can't do it, what *does* provide that sense of underlying contentment and satisfaction in life? Moment-to-moment *living*. The current moment—the nonjudgmental, unfiltered, pure experience of life.

You get the most from your experience of life when your personal thinking is relatively quiet and you are present in the moment, allowing life to unfold in front of you. You can experience more joy folding laundry or filing papers than going on your dream vacation if you are fully *in* life and not just *thinking about* life. Being deeply in the moment rather than in your personal thinking is *living*. There is a good feeling there. It's where lasting satisfaction is born—and it is where habits die.

Children are an excellent example of living life to the fullest. Although they live in the same world of ebbing and flowing thought that adults do, they don't *think about* their thinking. Their thinking comes and goes unimpeded, because they aren't in the way of it. As such, they find themselves having a more pure experience of life as it unfolds in front of them.

Young children excel at living because they aren't lost in thought. They are so engrossed in what is right in front of them that they experience joy in nearly everything. I see this with my own children all the time. Things adults would typically find monotonous—long car rides, standing in line, grocery shopping—are often a party to them. They are so engaged in the sights and sounds around them that they naturally see the fun in what's there. They aren't stuck in thinking about what's next or where they would rather be, so they are free to love the moment they are in. They place bets on which line will move fastest when we're in line at the store; they play "I Spy" or make silly faces at other customers at the bank; they imagine our car is a spaceship headed to the moon on road trips. Because they are *in* life as it is, they experience loads of joy in it.

When you grew up and began getting wrapped up in your personal thinking, you stopped being *in* the world the way you were as a kid. Since you weren't experiencing the same degree of delight and wonderment in the moment-to-moment unfolding of everyday life, you sought out ways to create more of those feelings.

And you promptly looked outside of yourself to do so. You looked past the car you were in or the grocery store you were walking through—*Delight and wonderment couldn't possibly be found there!*—and you thought bigger. You set your sights on something bigger, something that would surely make you feel great, like having the right jeans, being friends with the right people, or throwing the perfect birthday party (you were an adolescent, after all). You undoubtedly saw that those goals may have been fun and satisfying in and of themselves but that they didn't provide the lasting delight you were searching for. So before you knew it, your mind landed on even bigger, better goals. Although none of those took you back to that childlike feeling you were chasing, you kept trying. There had to be a way to get back there.

There is, and it's not going to be in anything you do. It's in *how you are*. It's in the feeling that comes from within when your mind is at ease and you are simply *living*. Setting out to accomplish things may make your life richer in many ways. It may bring you success and money and help you be a productive member of society, but it will not bring you lasting fulfillment on a moment-to-moment basis.

Ending your habit won't be the magic pill either, although it sure can help you live a nicer life. Like any accomplishment or positive change you might make, becoming habit-free will be very exciting for a while. It may be a source of gratitude for a long time after—I still experience frequent feelings of awe and profound gratitude that I am no longer stuck in my old habits. But after the everyday excitement wears off, you could find yourself habit-free and back to living from your head. For the deeper feelings of connection, purpose, love, and joy that all humans crave, you'll have to practice *living*—meaningfully being in the world as it is, rather than imagining or striving for the world you want it to be.

That's easier than it sounds, because when your personal thinking settles and you relax into the present moment, you will discover that life, as it is right now, is pretty amazing.

Final Thoughts

Trying to conceive my first child wasn't as easy as I had expected it to be.

Eighteen months and eighteen negative pregnancy tests in, I was beyond discouraged. I was beside myself in frustration and fear. One day, a very wise friend asked me something I'll never forget: "What's the absolute best that could come of this struggle?"

The only "best thing" I could possibly imagine is that I would get pregnant, preferably that night, if I had my way. I hit a major blind spot trying to answer her question. *What does she mean? What's the best that could come of it? Isn't it obvious?*

It was inconceivable to me (pardon the pun) that those eighteen negative pregnancy tests could be *positive* in any way. I'd feel positive when the test was positive; it was that simple. That's when my suffering would end. An end to the suffering was as good as I could imagine it getting.

My wise friend pushed me a bit. "I know this is a hard time for you," she said, "but you really can't see any bigger than that? A baby and an end to the suffering—that's all you've got?"

Over the next few days, her questions replayed in my head. Somehow, by sheer grace, light found its way to my blind spot.

Fleeting thoughts of the good in the struggle floated across my mind. I thought about some of the close moments I'd shared with my husband in that year and a half, how our fertility issues had helped me think of us as a team. I thought about the healthier physical and emotional changes I had made in my life in an attempt to make it easier to conceive.

My struggles had forced me to look inward at how my own thinking—not the presence or absence of a baby—was creating my moment-to-moment experience in life. I remembered insights and growth—*lots* of insights and growth, actually—that may not have occurred had I not been suffering in that way.

I would have traded all of that personal growth for a healthy baby in a heartbeat. But at least I was finally seeing a broader view of things. I didn't have the option of trading my insights for a baby, so I had to take what I got, and what I got was starting to look much better than it previously had. It was a doorway to a richer life in many ways.

What was I saying! A year and a half of suffering gave me a richer life? But it did. Once I saw that, I couldn't "unsee" it. To my friend's question, the absolute best that could come of my situation was that I could actually be *better off* for my struggle. This entire ordeal could have happened *for* me instead of *to* me. Even better, it might not be about *me* at all. Other people might be better off for my struggle. I couldn't wrap my head around how that might look, but I deeply felt that it was a distinct possibility.

Once I saw it in infertility, I saw it in my eating issues, and my professional uncertainty, and my childhood. I don't mean to make it sound as if every problem suddenly looked like a blessing, and life instantly looked perfect. That was definitely not my experience. But I did start to entertain the idea that difficult things happen *for* us and that our wisdom is always there, even when it looks like it's not. And as I did, the blessings in my struggles started popping out of the woodwork.

My wish for you is that the habit that brought you to this book someday comes to look like a blessing in disguise, that perhaps what was *in* the way *is* the way to a richer life for you as well. Maybe the suffering you've experienced around your habit is a doorway for you too—a doorway to a bigger view of what it means to be human.

Maybe you've caught even a tiny glimpse of the infinite creative potential that lies within you—or of the innate health that is fundamental to you, regardless of the human experience you're having. If you have, your suffering may have all been worth it.

Maybe you have come to see yourself in a more spiritual way—less fixed, not as tightly bound to ideas about your identity or your "addictive personality." Maybe you've seen that you actually are doing the best you can in every moment, even when your best falls short of what you'd like it to be.

Perhaps you're seeing that you are not too stubborn, self-sabotaging, or unwilling to change—that you are not too far gone. You've simply found yourself caught up in the storm, having temporarily lost sight of the calm in the middle. You're no different from any other human on earth in that way.

Hopefully, you're beginning to see that you are not your habits, thoughts, urges, emotions, or behaviors. Those things occur within you, but they are not you.

Maybe you're also catching on to the fact that insight, not specific behavioral techniques or prescriptions, is what will set you free. Behavior takes care of itself when you see a deeper truth.

I hope that you have a feel for how self-correcting everything in life truly is. You don't need to fight or change or fix or figure out nearly as much as it may appear that you do. When it looks like the end of your habit is all on you, dependent upon the "right" mindset or actions, that only means that you have a lot on your mind. When you feel better, you'll see more clearly.

If any of these is your experience, I'd say your habit has served you well. It has broken you open to a far more peaceful, meaningful experience of life. You're being pointed back toward the truth of who you are. Your habit just might have been a gift that will someday far outweigh the negative impact it had.

I wouldn't be the least bit surprised.

Acknowledgments

I would like to thank Dr. William Pettit, Dr. Mark Howard, and Phil Hughes for their thoughtful comments on early drafts of this manuscript. Your suggestions, and the conversations each of you were willing to have with me around the ideas here, helped me see things more deeply and share them more clearly.

I would also like to acknowledge the clients I've been honored to work with over the years, especially those whose stories are represented in this book. I know that your honesty and openness will help many, many people.

Finally, thank you to Kathryn Hansen, Jack Trimpey, and the late Sydney Banks for sharing your insights and ideas with the world. Your understanding helped me to be free of my habits and experience a new level of freedom across the board.

References

Banks, Sydney. 1998. *The Missing Link: Reflections on Philosophy and Spirit*. Auburn, WA: Lone Pine.

———. 2007. *The Enlightened Gardener Revisited*. Auburn, WA: Lone Pine.

Beck, Martha. 2008. *Steering by Starlight: The Science and Magic of Finding Your Destiny*. Emmaus, PA: Rodale Books.

Begley, Sharon. 2007. *Train Your Mind, Change Your Brain: How a New Science Reveals Our Extraordinary Potential to Transform Ourselves*. New York: Ballantine Books.

Carr, Allen. 2004. *Allen Carr's Easy Way to Stop Smoking*. New York: Sterling.

Doidge, Norman. 2007. *The Brain That Changes Itself: Stories of Personal Triumph from the Frontiers of Brain Science*. London: Penguin Books.

Hansen, Kathryn. 2011. *Brain over Binge: Why I Was Bulimic, Why Conventional Therapy Didn't Work, and How I Recovered for Good.* Columbus, GA: Camellia.

Johnson, Amy. 2013. *Being Human: Essays on Thoughtmares, Bouncing Back, and Your True Nature.* Chicago: Inner Wellness.

Katie, Byron. 2006. *I Need Your Love—Is That True? How to Stop Seeking Love, Approval, and Appreciation and Start Finding Them Instead.* New York: Three Rivers Press.

Kühn, Simone, and Marcel Brass. 2009. "Retrospective Construction of the Judgment of Free Choice." *Consciousness and Cognition* 18, no. 1: 12–21.

Schwartz, Jeffrey, and Sharon Begley. 2002. *The Mind and the Brain: Neuroplasticity and the Power of Mental Force.* New York: HarperCollins.

Trimpey, Jack. 1996. *Rational Recovery: The New Cure for Substance Addiction.* New York: Pocket Books.

Wegner, Daniel. 1989. *White Bears and Other Unwanted Thoughts: Suppression, Obsession, and the Psychology of Mental Control.* New York: Viking/Penguin.

Amy Johnson, PhD, is a master life coach who works with clients worldwide through coaching programs, workshops, and retreats. She is author of *Being Human*. Johnson has been a regularly featured expert on *The Steve Harvey Show* and www.oprah.com, as well as in *The Wall Street Journal* and *Self* magazine. She has devoted a large portion of her coaching practice to helping people end unwanted habits. Visit the author at www.dramyjohnson.com.

Photo by Robin Lieb

Foreword writer **Mark Howard, PhD**, is founder of the Three Principles Institute in Burlingame, CA. He is a licensed psychologist, and recognized as one of the pioneers who first brought the Three Principles into the field of psychology. Since 1982, Howard has been teaching private clients, families, business professionals, and mental health practitioners about the principles. He continues to mentor and train health professionals in the Three Principles, and has dedicated his life to bringing peace, well-being, and happiness to humankind.

MORE BOOKS

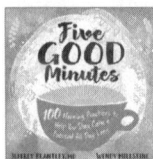

FIVE GOOD MINUTES
100 Morning Practices to Help You Stay
Calm and Focused All Day Long
978-1684036196 / US $19.95

THE DAILY RELAXER
Relax Your Body, Calm Your Mind, and
Refresh Your Spirit
978-1684036226 / US $14.95

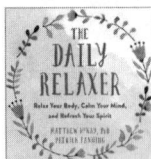

JUST ONE THING
Developing a Buddha Brain One Simple
Practice at a Time
978-1684036172 / US $16.95

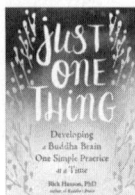

LEAVE YOUR MIND BEHIND
The Everyday Practice of Finding Stillness
Amid Rushing Thoughts
978-1684036189 / US $16.95

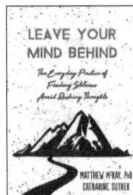

WOMEN WHO WORRY TOO MUCH
How to Stop Worry and Anxiety from
Ruining Relationships, Work, and Fun
978-1684036202 / US $18.95

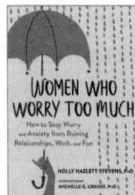